Shabbtai Zvi, 1669

Grape harvest in Rishon le Zion, Palestine, ca. 1925

Newsstand in Berlin,
June 1935

C.V. Zeitung

ALLGEMEINE ZEITUNG DES JUDENTUMS

Das Schaufenster

JÜDISCHE RUNDSCHAU

BERLIN

Zurück zum Jude-Sein!

„Gesetz, nach dem wir angetreten..."

Israelitisches

Familienblatt

Die große Chance

Der Katholik

Sonntagszeitung im Geist und Dienst Katholischer Aktion

„...und du wirst das Antlitz der Erde erneuern"

View down the Judengasse in Frankfurt, ca. 1860

Bertha Pappenheim, 1889

David Friedländer,
ca. 1788

Paul Ehrlich in his study, ca. 1910

Stories
of an Exhibition

Two Millennia of German Jewish History

Jewish Museum Berlin
Two Millennia of German Jewish History

Contents

Foreword

The Jewish Museum Berlin is opening its doors to visitors for a journey through two millennia of German Jewish history. Like its architecture, the content of this new museum is unique.

At the beginning of the 21st century, important changes are taking place in Germany. Among other developments, the Jewish communities in Germany have incontrovertibly assumed an established position in public affairs. Nevertheless, the only contact many non-Jewish Germans have with Jews and Judaism is in history class, where they are confronted with this theme primarily in connection with the persecution and murder of Jews by the National Socialist regime. The history of Jews in Germany involves more than this alone: we now look back over many tumultuous centuries of common history, a history full of progress and fresh starts as well as catastrophe.

The permanent exhibition of the Jewish Museum Berlin sharpens our focus on this history, which continues to shape our society even today. In contrast to most other Jewish museums, which present the

evolution of the Jewish religion separately from the general historical continuum, this exhibition interweaves the threads of intellectual and religious history with the political, cultural, and societal developments affecting German history in a broader manner. This perspective should help make clear that what we understand to be "German" culture—a concept defined by geography, language, and shared cultural values—has always been, and today, under changed conditions, continues to be the result of cross-pollination and synthesis between diverse currents and influences. This museum brings to life the significant contributions that Jews have made to the formation of German culture. A national museum for German Jewish history in the capital of Berlin will help orient us in the search for an understanding of ourselves as Germans and help us answer the questions that engross our society today.

Since assuming his post as director of the Jewish Museum Berlin in 1998, Michael Blumenthal has demonstrated that this museum, in addition to its educational goals, must take account of its political impact. The mission of this museum touches upon learning processes that belong to the sphere of political education: respect and recognition for minorities and tolerance in the sense of appreciating difference as a necessary condition both of democracy and of a culture increasingly characterized by diversity. The German government, on both state and federal levels, has supported the Jewish Museum in its scope and purpose. At the beginning of 2001, the museum became an independent foundation under the aegis of the federal government.

The Jewish Museum Berlin makes a decisive contribution to our historical consciousness, our responsibility as a nation, and Germany's cultural landscape. I wish all of us exciting discoveries and vivid dialogues with our history, its material, and its personal witnesses.

State Minister
Prof. Dr. Julian Nida-Rümelin
Federal Government Commissioner for Cultural Affairs
and the Media

Welcome to the Jewish Museum Berlin

The Jewish Museum Berlin is no ordinary museum. As a major institution of memory, it occupies a unique place in Germany's capital city. As a national institution supported by the Federal Government, the State of Berlin, all political parties, and a broad cross-section of the public, its mission has socio-political meaning that far transcends the story it tells of the 2000-year history of German Jewry. It symbolizes, in fact, a widely shared determination to confront the past and to apply its lessons to societal problems of today and tomorrow.

In depicting the ups and downs of the relationship between Jews and non-Jews in Germany, the museum illustrates what becomes possible when religious, cultural or ethnic minorities are able to contribute their unique talents to national life—and how terrible the consequences for all can be when intolerance and prejudice prevail. Together with its collection and archive, its departments of education and research, the Rafael Roth Learning Center, and the Leo Baeck Institute, the Jewish Museum Berlin is dedicated to depicting German history and explaining Jewish culture, while providing a forum for study, discussion and the interchange of ideas.

The relevance of this work to the universal challenge of promoting tolerance toward minorities in a globalized world and to their integration into national life is as clear as it is obvious.

Daniel Libeskind's architectural masterpiece symbolizes the central elements of this mission. The fact that this institution occupies so central a place in the German capital is especially meaningful.

A Jewish Museum in Berlin

As far back as the 1970s, a small group of Jewish and non-Jewish Berliners first conceived of the idea of establishing a Jewish Museum in Berlin. Two principal motivations guided their thinking. Though the post-war Jewish community was very small, Berlin had once been home to a large number of Jewish citizens, and the survivors and their friends did not want the lives and achievements of their erstwhile fellow citizens to be forgotten. Secondly, they wanted future generations of Berliners to be reminded that the distinguished history of their city prior to Hitler could not be understood without taking account of the once vibrant Jewish presence there.

The original plans evolved slowly and provoked vigorous, often emotional debate. Should it be

*The Jewish Museum Berlin: Kollegienhaus
and Libeskind building*

a historical museum, or one devoted to Jewish religion and culture? Should it focus on Berlin alone,
or on all German Jews? Would it be a department of
the City Museum, or an entirely new and separate
institution? Was a new building required, or would
the museum be housed in an existing one—and how
would the entire project be financed?

Today's Jewish Museum has moved far
beyond these early debates. In the meantime, the
wall between the two Germanys has disappeared and
Berlin is once again the capital of a reunited single
country. Not surprisingly, therefore, when the Jewish
Museum opened its doors in 2001, it was a vastly different institution with a wider scope than the one
envisaged by its original proponents. Far from being
a department of a city museum, the visitor will encounter an independent national institution, the

largest Jewish museum in Europe. Its mission encompasses the entire history of German-speaking
Jewry since Roman times.

Its twin homes are an architectural treasure
with its own deeply symbolic significance—the start-
ling structure created by the American architect
Daniel Libeskind and the beautiful baroque former
Berlin court building to which it is joined underground. The one stands in stark contrast to the
other, yet both are dramatically linked as one.

In the first post-war decades, the traumatic
impact of the persecution and murder of European
Jewry by Germany's rulers was overpowering.
Neither the generation of perpetrators and bystan-
ders on the German side, nor the handful of Jewish
survivors living in Germany were able to communi-
cate honestly and to confront the meaning and

lessons of the terrible events of the past. Perhaps it required a new generation of Germans, those born after 1945 or too young to have played a role in Nazi Germany, and a larger and more secure Jewish presence to openly face what had occurred.

The opening of the Jewish Museum Berlin within an evolving memorial landscape demonstrates that the time to do so has now arrived. Thus, this museum is the result of the effort of subsequent generations in Germany to examine the past in the knowledge that there can be no future without memory .

A Museum for Everyone

The Museum's permanent exhibition attempts to tell the story of German Jewry in all its dimensions. The aim is to do so fairly, yet in an interesting and lively way, utilizing the full range of modern exhibit-

ing techniques. We want the exhibits to be historically accurate, yet we have also aimed to appeal to all visitor interests and backgrounds, with special emphasis on the many young people we hope to attract. At the same time, those who wish to delve more deeply into the subject matter will find analytical scope for their interests in our archives, the interactive Rafael Roth Learning Center and the Leo Baeck Institute. A program of temporary exhibitions is planned for future years. Each of these will concentrate in greater depth on specific aspects of German Jewish history. A cultural and educational program focused on the arts, music, literature, and Jewish cultural heritage will serve to widen the interest and knowledge of visitors.

Many generous contributors—German as well as international—have supported us. Many have sent us valuable artifacts and historic memorabilia and some of these have become part of the permanent exhibition. Others will be shown in subsequent years, as the exhibition is expanded and temporary exhibits are added.

All visitors should find something of interest in what they encounter. Our aim is to engage everyone in the telling of a dramatic story and in reflecting on its meaning for the future.

The Jewish Museum Berlin is meant to be a museum for everyone: young and old, German and non-German, Jewish and non-Jewish. As the museum grows, evolves and matures, its exhibitions and cultural programs will, we hope, contribute to the expanding of knowledge and to the building of a tolerant and peaceful society.

W. Michael Blumenthal

Festivities at the Mosse's, painting by Anton von Werner, 1899

*Projection of the
Certificate of Citizenship for
Moses Isaac, January 26, 1813,
from the archives of the
Jewish Museum Berlin,
on the facade of the
Libeskind building.*

*Installation by
Jenny Holzer,
February 2001*

The Vision and the Exhibitions

In the telling of the history of one cultural group, the German Jews, within the context of broader German history, the Jewish Museum Berlin confronts one of the most taxing stories of world history. The Museum talks of a relationship among neighbors, the cultural border between Jewish and non-Jewish citizens. It is a place that examines the way this border has opened and closed, disappeared and reappeared over time. The Museum looks at the movements and exchanges across this border and at the frictions in this relationship, which have proven to be calamitous at times.

This history spans some two millennia, from the time the first Jews came into ancient Germania to the present day. It covers the many achievements of Jews in Germany. However, this story also includes an ongoing record of anti-Judaism and anti-Semitism, culminating in the Nazi era—the darkest side of this relationship. With the Holocaust, the Museum addresses a time when the German Jews were systematically deprived of their civil rights, persecuted and murdered—a time in which so much that defines humanity in a nation became lost.

This story tells of the dangers of intolerance and bigotry. A visit to the Museum is therefore no easy decision—visitors could so easily put aside a trip to the Jewish Museum Berlin in favor of something far less demanding and more entertaining.

With this in mind, the Museum attempts to make the visit a special one. An encounter with this history might be difficult, thought-provoking and challenging, yet the visit will offer a rewarding and positive experience. This is a place of welcome, a place of interesting and engaging exhibits and programs. To increase the impact of the exhibits, we are making appropriate use of the most modern interactive and digitalized exhibition technology alongside the more traditional forms. Contemporary artists join the Museum in developing parts of our story.

It is the hope of the Museum that it can make a difference, touching people in a way that will affect their thinking and even, perhaps, their actions. Our first priority, therefore, is to present this history to the younger generations, that is, to the children and parents of the German family. The Museum is also committed to the international visitor, and all information is presented both in German and in English.

In order to tell this story accurately and in all its richness, the Museum commits itself to being a place of scholarship. All that it does and presents is based on the research of both its own staff and the broader academic community. All academic concepts have been subject to review and comment by a board of senior academic historians from universities in Germany and overseas.

der Inhaber dieses der
vor der Polizei-Obrigkeit seines Wohnorts erklärt
hat, daß er den Namen
Namen ferner beibehalten will, so wird in Gemäßheit des §. 4.
März 1812 hierdurch bezeuget, daß der
und seine Nachkommen
Preußische Einländer und
angenommen und überall
Januar 1813

The Narrative

To achieve these purposes, the Jewish Museum Berlin presents a narrative that is broadly chronological, with the visitor moving from very early times to the present. The story follows the life of individual protagonists and communities living among their neighbors—their way of life, their privations and their achievements, and the slow path toward emancipation and equality, strewn as it was with obstacles. Always close at hand, however, and a constant part of the history of the Jews in Germany, is the theme of prejudice and persecution.

Jewish history is one of dispersal by migration and expulsion. In Roman times, the Jewish people had spread out across many parts of the known world. They acted as traders in the commodities of the time and developed great skills in languages. They visited countries as far away as India and perhaps China, often as emissaries for potentates. One, Isaak of Narbonne, returned over the Alps with an African elephant, a gift from the caliph of Baghdad to the court of Charlemagne.

Our story begins as the Jews, having moved through the Mediterranean, settled in ancient Germania following the Roman legions. The earliest record tells of an organized Jewish community in Cologne in the year 321, when Constantine the Great, the first Christian Emperor of Rome, issued a codex to the authorities of the City of Cologne, revoking the exemption of Jews from costly honorary offices.

Virtually nothing is known of Jewish settlement in the 'Dark Ages,' but by the 10th century, thriving Jewish enclaves existed along the Rhine river in Speyer, Mainz and Worms and other medieval towns. From this point onwards, Jews have been a constant presence in the life and history of Germany.

An amazing woman of the Jewish community in the late 17th and early 18th century, Glikl bas Judah Leib, left a memoir that records her life as an accomplished business woman and trader. Other lives were more difficult. The rural poor and the Jewish beggars suffered great difficulties. Many had no right to settle in one place and were dependent on the welfare of established Jewish communities and families. A minority within the minority, the court Jews, rose above this. With their skills in commerce and finance, they found privileged positions at the royal courts. The gains were great—as were the dangers, when, for various reasons, they fell from favor.

It was the philosopher Moses Mendelssohn and his circle that demonstrated that German Jews could maintain their religion while opening themselves to German culture at the same time. Politically and socially, the struggle for emancipation began with these thinkers of the Jewish Enlightenment. This process initiated dramatic external as well as internal reforms for the Jewish communities. The exhibition also examines the everyday life of Jews in Germany—religious observances and changing philosophies, rites of passage, education and the role of families.

In the 19th century, Jews in Germany could point with confidence to their increasing status as citizens and their position within the developing bourgeois society. There was still much to be achieved, but Jewish citizens were contributing greatly to the growth of industry and science as well as to the arts and civil society. The "Jewish Renaissance" was expressed in a vibrant and creative cultural life. New visions developed, offering multiple

Bertha Pappenheim as Glikl, portrait by Leopold Pilichowski, before 1925

models for a Jewish identity and sense of self—such as the twin utopias of the return to an authentic community in the East and the political vision of an autonomous Jewish state. Jewish citizens joined the German war efforts in large numbers and with considerable loss of life.

However, this progress was to be brought to nothing by the rise of National Socialism. Beginning in 1933, the German Jews were forced to react to ever increasing restrictions and persecution. Many went into exile, fleeing to all corners of the world. When the deportation of those remaining began in 1941, some chose the dangerous course of going underground. Some Jews survived to the end of the war; nonetheless, around 200,000 German Jews were brutally murdered.

Part of this story from 1933 to 1945 is told in the Axes, the underground area of corridors through which the Museum exhibits are entered. The architect Daniel Libeskind contructed this part of the building to offer an encounter with the fate of the Jews of Germany during this twelve-year period. A series of spaces conveys specific messages—the Axis of the Holocaust ending in the Holocaust Tower, the Axis of Exile leading to the Garden of Exile, and the Stairs of Continuity that guide the way into the exhibition spaces above ground. Here, in the Axes, history is told through the stories of individuals and families swept up in these events.

At the end of World War II, German Jewry was dispersed or murdered. But those few remaining, together with returning emigrants and survivors from Eastern Europe, began re-establishing Jewish communities. Most, however, regarded life in the country of the perpetrators as temporary—their destinations were Israel, the United States and other parts of the world. By the 1960s, though, some began

unpacking their suitcases. After the fall of the Berlin Wall, the growing communities were joined by refugees from the countries of the former Soviet Union. Today, the Jewish community in Germany probably numbers some 100,000 people.

The current exhibits of the Jewish Museum Berlin can in no way offer a final word on the history of Jewish life in Germany. This is an evolving story that the Museum will continue to develop through the years. A continuous and vigorous public debate accompanies the telling of the fate of Jews in Germany, and the Jewish Museum Berlin offers a forum for these voices. An understanding of this history plays an important role in the definition of Germany as a modern and democratic nation today.

Daniel Libeskind's Concept for the Building

The building of the Jewish Museum Berlin is now firmly established as one of the masterpieces of contemporary architecture and a work of art in its own right. In very large part, Daniel Libeskind's architecture has achieved this reputation by bringing together and infusing within an award-winning design emblematic statements arising from the history of Jews in Germany.

These are expressed as highly developed design elements. The building's fragmented form and industrial material, the jagged lines of the windows and the lines that cross ceilings and floors, the extensive garden, and the use of the concept of "underground," all evoke a response in the visitor that draws upon and informs his or her under-

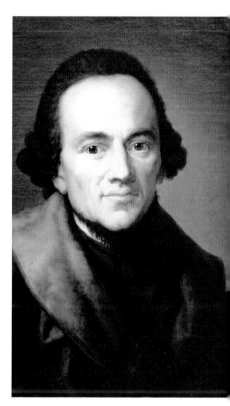

Moses Mendelssohn, portrait by August Theodor Kaselowsky after Anton Graff, ca. 1855

standing of this history. The building is cut through by an empty space, the Void. In the Void, Libeskind symbolically recognizes the destruction of European Jewry—the absence, the empty spaces that exist in German and European society.

This is one of those rare places where the architecture and the narrative of the museum accord, where each supports and strengthens the other. We don't have the traditional series of neutral and malleable gallery spaces. Rather, the building offers a unique museum opportunity where architectural philosophy and exhibition concept arise out of the same approach to the same subject.

This approach is reflected throughout the Museum. There are places which we call "Libeskind moments," where the architecture comes to the fore as the principle statement unfettered by objects and exhibition. In the Axes, it is the emotional impact of the underground corridors that dominate, and the exhibitions touch the architecture softly.

The Voids have offered a particularly fruitful site for co-operation among Daniel Libeskind, the staff, and the contemporary artists Menashe Kadishmann in the Memory Void and Via Lewandowsky with the Gallery of the Missing to integrate the architectural concept with the Museum's mission.

Even in the most standard of the exhibition areas, Libeskind's windows frame portions of the exhibition and form points about which exhibition designers Würth & Winderoll have focused a particular theme.

Würth & Winderoll—The Exhibition Designers

The exhibitions in the Jewish Museum Berlin have been designed and constructed by the design firm of Würth & Winderoll and their allied construction company, Strand Ausstellungsrealisation GmbH. This group was engaged because of their experience, the quality of their design, their ability to build strong partnerships with museum staff, and their record of working with and responding to market research data.

At the head of Würth & Winderoll are Petra Winderoll, designer, and Klaus Würth, project manager, a husband and wife team resident in Seefeld, outside of Munich.

Their firm has completed an impressive array of museum design contracts. These include the Haus der Geschichte der Bundesrepublik Deutschland in Bonn, the successful national history museum that presents German post-war history in a highly engaging manner. They have also been responsible for redesigning the Bayerisches Nationalmuseum in Munich and the Museum für Kunst und Kulturgeschichte in Dortmund. In the nineteen years the firm has been in existence, they have completed over 200 museum design and construction projects.

Würth & Winderoll have a particular facility for making intimate, engaging moments for the visitor. They create magical instances in which individual visitors are removed from the narrative of history and drawn in close to a private focus on a telling fact or a resonant object. Their sense of the visitor's needs means that their design offers

changes of pace, mood and focal length—all the
while maintaining the momentum of a broad sweep
through time. They are skillful at providing simulta-
neous levels of experience; thus, while parents might
be studying virulent anti-Semitic handbills in a
drawer, their children will be busy exploring special
pathways through the building's architecture. The
designers have provided the Museum with a series of
carefully managed high points, followed by periods
for rest, contemplation, and analysis.

Stories of an Exhibition

We hope that our audience, both the visitors of the
exhibitions and the readers of this book, will engage
in a lively and inspiring interaction with German
Jewish history. In the pages of this book, we are
telling stories that allow individual protagonists to
step out from the panorama of history. A scholarly
catalogue for the Jewish Museum Berlin is in preparation—in the "Stories of an Exhibition," we
would like to introduce you to indicative voices and
objects that open different perspectives on the
complex history of Jews in Germany.

Ken Gorbey

*opposite and above:
Designs for the
permanent exhibition*

Two Millennia
of German Jewish History

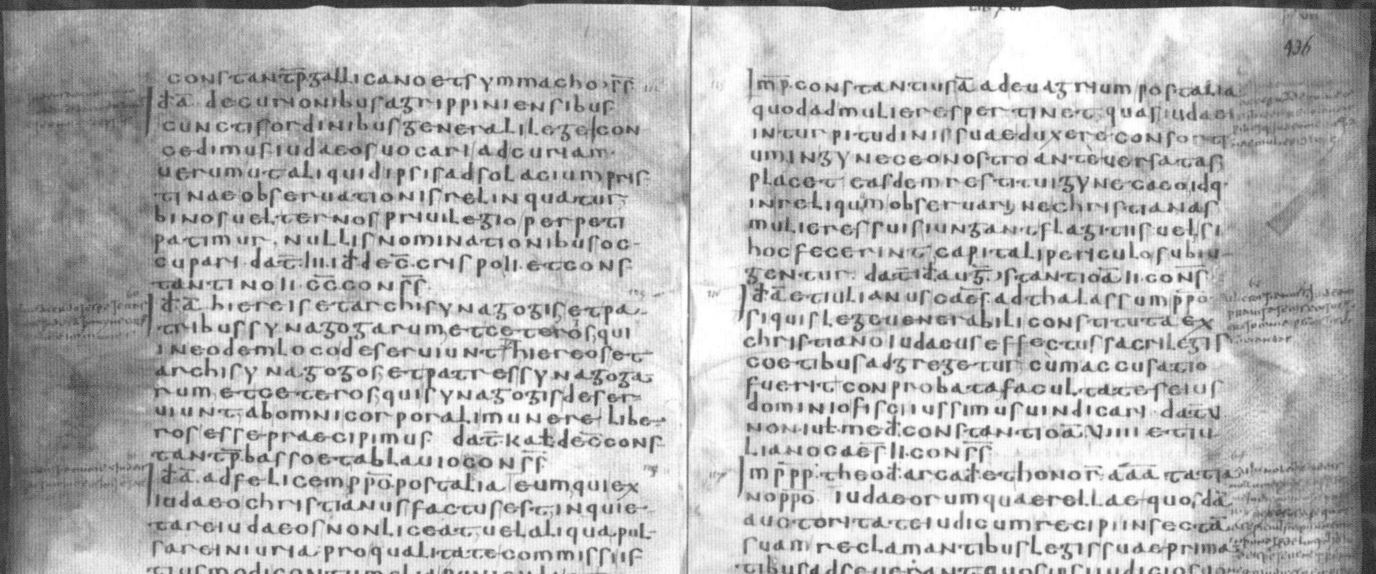

Copy of a decree issued by the Emperor Constantine on January 11, 321 C.E. (Codex Theodosianus)

"Children of Israel"

The Diaspora in Europe

In the year 321, the Roman emperor Constantine sent a decree to the magistrate of Cologne that read: "By general law, all authorities are permitted to appoint Jews to the papal court." This document, that revoked the exemption of Jews from costly honorary offices, is considered to be the oldest written testimony of what has since become a nearly 2000 year-old German Jewish history, the earliest evidence of Jewish communities in the Germanic provinces of the Roman Empire. In other European regions, for instance in Spain and Italy, there were a multitude of Jewish settlements at that time, whose inhabitants lived their tradition in the midst of an environment dominated by different faiths. What, however, had induced these people to leave a "Holy Land" which played such a central role in Jewish thought and belief, and to move to foreign lands?

According to the Jewish calendar, which dates the creation of the world at 3760 before the Common Era and looks back over a span of millennia, it was already the year 4081 when the Roman emperor gave the "decurions of Cologne" his instructions for dealing with *rabbis** and the heads of *synagogues*. The Biblical record, based as it was chiefly on Moses, may not always hold up to historical examination, and the borders between legend and truth are often blurred. Yet a retrospect of this history can illuminate the cultural and religious constants, as well as the changes, in the Jewish sense of self and of the world throughout the centuries.

The Promised Land

From antiquity onwards, the fate of the Jews has been irrevocably interwoven with the promised land "Israel," yet at the same time Jewish history is a history of the *Diaspora*, of a life as a religious minority scattered throughout all the corners of the

Silver Hanukkah lamp, Berlin, 1779

world. It was only during one short phase around 1000 B.C.E. in the time of King David that a unified country with the holy city of Jerusalem at its center existed in Palestine. The memory of this nourished a longing for a return through many centuries, becoming a significant theological and social element of Judaism and serving among other things as a substantiation for the establishment of the state of Israel in 1948.

In Palestine itself, called "Canaan" in the Hebrew Bible, the "land of milk and honey," the homeland of the Jews has always been a matter of dispute. "Israel" was originally the name of the people chosen by God whose history begins with the "patriarch" Abraham, his son Isaac and his offspring Jacob. In search of the one true God, "Abraham left Ur in Chaldea to enter the land of Canaan" (Genesis, 11:31). What is here portrayed as a peaceful settlement was in truth a long and complex process. In a manner similar to the group surrounding Abraham, numerous Semitic nomads left the Syrian and Arabian deserts for the fertile cultivated landscape of Canaan in the 20th century B.C.E., initially settling as farmers and partial nomads. In Canaan, Jacob changed his name to Israel; his twelve sons are considered to be the forefathers of the twelve tribes of Israel. When a devastating famine broke out two generations later, Abraham's progeny fled to Egypt; as unwelcome strangers, however, they soon ended up in bondage. Long years of forced labor and slavery resulted in their growing together into a group, a "people"; towards the end of the 12th century B.C.E., they rebelled against the oppression. Under the leadership of Moses, the "children of Israel" finally left Egypt, and, as it is written in the *Torah*, after forty years of wandering through the desert, they arrived once again in the "promised land."

The two areas of the empire now formed, Israel in the north and Judah in the south, continued however to remain under threat through

* The words set in italics are featured in the glossary at the back of this book.

internal disputes and powerful outside enemies. King David was the first to unify both parts of the country into one kingdom. Jerusalem, the "City of David," became the capital of the empire and its central holy shrine shortly thereafter with the erection of the magnificent first temple under the rule of David's son Solomon. Once wandering with the tribes, God had now acquired a permanent residence.

This brief heyday drew to an end with Solomon's death in 926 B.C.E. Ten of the twelve tribes of Israel revolted against Solomon's successor Rehoboam, banding together to form the new kingdom of Israel in the north of the country. Only the tribes Judah (Jehudah) and Benjamin remained loyal to the king and founded the kingdom of Judah in the south, with Jerusalem as its capital. Following an eventful history of both empires, the north was conquered in 722 B.C.E. by the Assyrians and the ten tribes were scattered or destroyed. In the southern empire Judah, however, which submitted to the Assyrian rule, peace and stability initially prevailed. Only the descendants of Judah survived—as the Jews.

Silver Hanukkah candelabrum by George Wilhelm Marggraff, Berlin, ca. 1776

Diaspora

The consolidation as a people continued as the Babylonians conquered the country in 586 B.C.E., destroyed the temple in Jerusalem, and deported a majority of the Jews to Babylonia. Because the "Promised Land" was lost, yet the exiles to a large extent kept to their own customs and habits in the foreign land, they withdrew into spirituality and religion, rallied around their prophets and teachers, and grew together into a community. Prayer took the place of the former sacrificial customs; the adherence to the religious commandments, the *mitzvot*, held the "House of Israel" together, and the shock of the expulsion became a central theological metaphor. The prophets Jeremiah and Ezekiel taught that the loss of the home country was less God's punishment than a test of their belief—

combined with the divine call to stand up for truth and justice, even under adverse circumstances, but to respect the rules of a foreign society at the same time. The *Talmud* later quotes God as saying: "Preserve your lips from every sin and misconduct, and I will be with you everywhere."

This message decisively influenced the Jewish sense of self during the Diaspora. Loyalty to the state one lived in, regardless of what circumstances were responsible for the fact, became a veritable religious duty. An attitude of this kind was destined to place religious life on a new foundation. The Torah was now read, explained, and made available to the members of the community on a regular basis; this no longer required a priest, but a teacher, a rabbi. Furthermore, the rabbi (literally "my teacher" in Hebrew) didn't need a temple, symbolizing God's residence, but rather a meeting place in which the community could actively take part in worship—a development in which prayer houses, synagogues, and liturgies found their beginnings.

When the Persian king Cyrus conquered Babylonia, he allowed the Jews to return to their homeland in 538 B.C.E. A more peaceful period began, and the Judaeans were able to retain self-administration and freedom of religion in their small state up until Hellenistic times. It was only after the early death of Alexander the Great in 323 B.C.E.

that Jerusalem once again came under the rule of various parties and was annexed to the kingdom of Syria. The temple, which had been built anew in the year 515 B.C.E., was desecrated, the Jewish religion violently suppressed. In 167 B.C.E., this finally led to a revolt of the "pious," the so-called Maccabean Wars under the leadership of Judas Maccabaeus; their happy outcome is celebrated to this day with the holiday of *Hanukkah*. For the following hundred years, the country lived in independence and prosperity until the Roman Empire extended its rule to Palestine.

Roman Rule

From 63 B.C.E. onwards, the Romans took over power in the country. Among the procurators, the brutal and corruptible Roman governors of Palestine, Pontius Pilate was certainly one of the most feared. As the brutality of the occupiers increased—hundreds were condemned to death by crucifixion, including Jesus of Nazareth—unrest and the desire for liberation grew. Armed resistance developed which the Roman Legions were only able to crush four years later in 70 C.E.: Jerusalem and the second temple were destroyed. Although further serious revolts took place in the years following, the last of which occurred under Bar Kokhba (132–135 C.E.), the Romans continued to hold the upper hand. Jerusalem became entirely Roman and the Jews were forbidden under threat of death to enter the city ever again. With this, the national core of Jewry was lost and the history of Israel as a people in Palestine came to an end.

The Middle East certainly remained a central focus of settlement. However, in the wake of the Roman Legions, voluntarily or otherwise, as slaves or as traders, large numbers of Jews had set foot in nearly all provinces of the Roman Empire. Set-

The oldest known Torah scroll from the Ashkenazic area, ca. 1300

The Jüdenstrasse near the City Hall in Berlin

tlements arose all around the Mediterranean basin, in the Balkans, in Italy, on the Iberian Peninsula, and in Gaul, for the most part along the ancient trading routes.

The emperor Constantine, who created the statutory regulations for dealings with Jews in 321, was to play a crucial role in the subsequent history of the Occident. Under his dominion, Christianity experienced a boom after many long years of the persecution of Christians. He himself had been christened on his deathbed so that Christianity could become the state religion of the Roman Empire. With Constantine, not only did the history of the tolerance of Christianity begin, but the history of the close bond between church and state, as well—and with it the history of the Christian as well as the Jewish Middle Ages.

Tradition and Change—
The Halakhah

The center of spiritual life in Judaism is not, as in other religions, formed by theology in the sense of pondering the nature of God and the beyond; rather, the practical application of the mitzvot, the commandments of the written Torah (the five books of Moses), stands at the heart of everyday life in the Jewish community. The rules of daily life are laid down in Jewish religious law, termed the *Halakhah*. Derived from the Hebrew verb "to go, to walk," the word "Halakhah" doesn't stress the legitimacy of the Torah as a book of rules, but rather refers to the path along which God leads people to a successful life.

The Teachings

Jewish religious law was collected and systematized in various codices. The Halakhah is not static and immutable, however, but rather a flexible instrument that takes into account human life and its needs and changes. Its foundation are the 613 commandments and proscriptions rabbis traditionally counted in the Bible. Debates on their individual application, how they could or should be observed in a respective historical context, in a specific location, and at a specific time have been taking place continuously throughout the centuries in the houses of learning. Initially passed on orally, such scholarly discussions were later transcribed and conserved in compilations of which the most well-known are the Jerusalemite (Palestinian) and the Babylonian Talmud. Due to their origins, they are termed "oral teachings" and serve as amendments to the Torah.

Contemporary kippot from the USA and Israel
underlay: Josef Caro, "Shulhan Arukh," Hanau, 1627

33

right:
Silver Torah pointer,
Nuremberg,
mid-19th century

center:
Silver Torah pointer,
Warsaw,
19th century

far right:
Torah crown,
partially gilded silver,
Berlin, ca. 1912

Mitzvot cards, 19th century

The Prepared Table

For practical usage, various codices exist which sum up the prevalent rabbinical decisions in concise form, preparing and presenting them in such a way that the lay person can use them on a daily basis. The *Shulhan Arukh* is considered to be the most famous reference book of the Halakhah. Shulhan Arukh literally means the "prepared table" which another, more educated person already laid and whose abundance can now be drawn from. The Shulhan Arukh was first published in 1565 by Josef Caro for the *Sephardic* world. In order to incorporate the Halakhic traditions of the *Ashkenazim*, Moses Isserles wrote a commentary called the *Mappah*—the tablecloth for the Sephardic table. In the four major movements of today's Judaism—Orthodox, Conservative, and Reform Judaism, as well as Reconstructionism—the Halakhah assumes a respectively different position and is interpreted in different ways.

*Jew at his studies,
illumination,
ca. 1470*

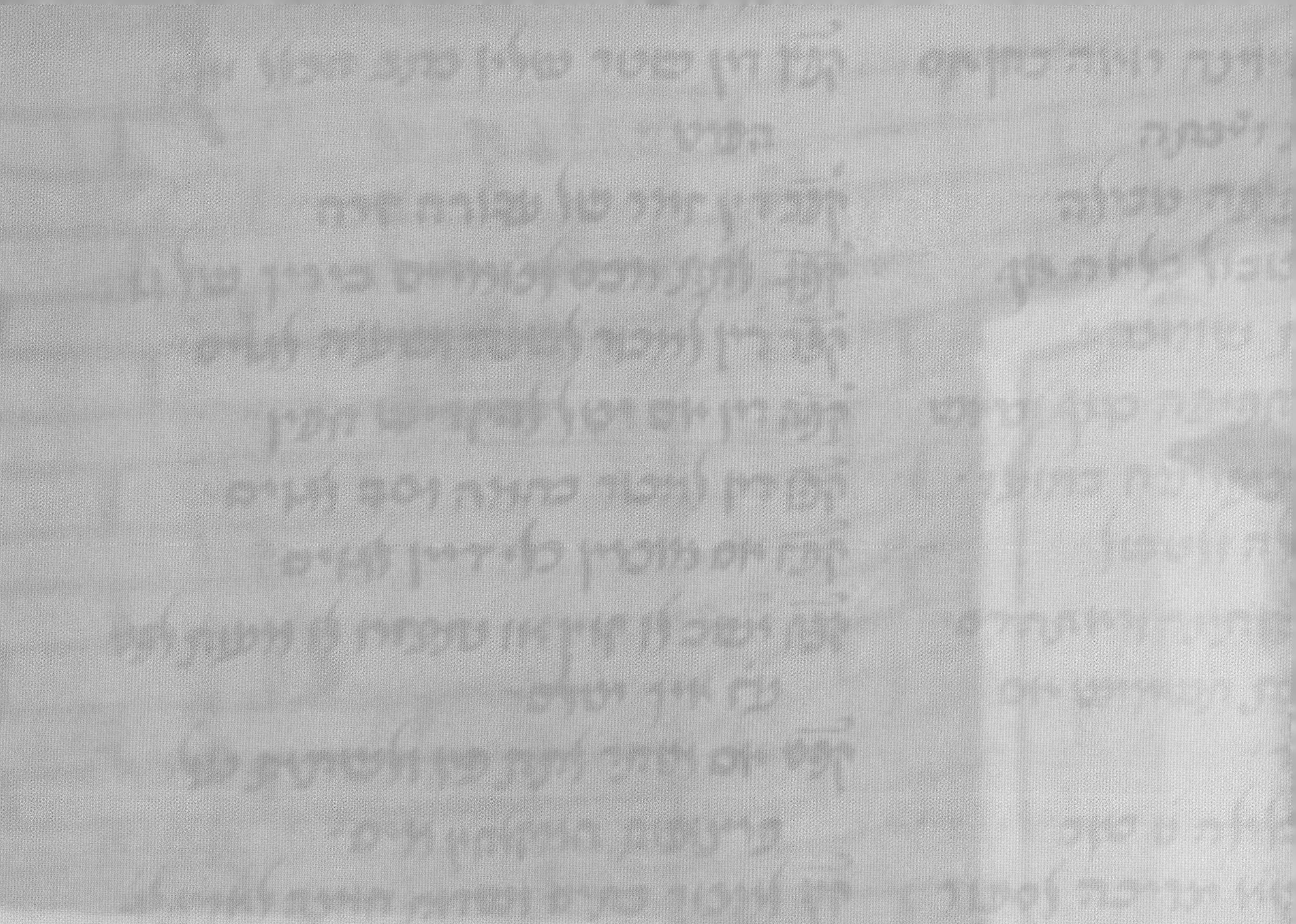

The World of Ashkenaz

Jewish Communities in the Middle Ages

With the conversion of Emperor Constantine to Christianity, the balance of power in Europe changed. The Christian clergy stepped onto the stage of world history; due to its close involvement with the ecclesiastically composed state, over the course of the following centuries it increasingly imposed a political and legal outsider role onto the Jews, who, in the religious diversity of the Roman Empire, had enjoyed equal rights. Shortly after Constantine's death, his successor Theodosius, the last emperor of the Roman Empire, stiffened the existing laws.

Yet, the Jewish religion continued to remain a religio licita, a religion permitted by the state which could be practiced under the formal protection of the Roman Empire. Despite all the Christian bells, symbols and processions which increasingly came to dominate the public arena, what separated them from the rest carried less

weight than what they had in common. Under the conditions of life at that time, Jews and Christians initially and for the most part dealt with each other as neighbors who traded with each other, who worked together, who were, in short, mutually dependent on one another.

Life in Ashkenaz

Jewish trading families had settled along the trade routes of the Rhine. Any new settlement was welcome to the secular and religious rulers, for every field that was cultivated, every house that was filled with life, every market place that developed into a city enhanced their renown and signified progress. Compared with other population groups, Jews often had skills and experience at their disposal which proved invaluable, for instance in setting up a state administration and expanding the trade sector.

Jewish boys had been learning how to read Hebrew from time immemorial in obedience of the divine commandment to study the Torah, while the majority of the Christians continued to remain illiterate for centuries. The Talmud—with all its stories about resolving arguments and breaking the law, about sizes and weights, compensation and defraudation, decrease in value and remuneration—not only instructed them in the ways of the world, but also imparted valuable skills for trade and business.

The ruling princes were quite happy to make use of these skills. Jews were highly esteemed both as doctors and as foreign merchants and seafarers who came close to holding a monopoly over Mediterranean trade in the 8th and 9th centuries, providing the royal and bishopric palaces with jewels, spices, perfumes, and other luxury goods. Their services as teachers and advisors were sought after, as

well: the story of the merchant Isaak of Narbonne, whom Charlemagne entrusted in 797 with a Christian legation, is legendary; his task was to lead them to Baghdad to the court of the caliph Harun ar-Rashid as a guide well-versed in both language and geography. Isaak was the only one not to perish from the strain of the journey, and five years later he returned to Aachen with an elephant by the name of Abulabaz, a gift from the caliph.

Under Charlemagne, king of the Franks and, from the year 800 on, the first emperor of the Holy Roman Empire, numerous Jewish communities were founded, and trade and the arts boomed. It was the era of royal Jewish safeguarding: Jews were placed on even legal footing with the Christians regarding economic questions. They were in charge of their own property, traded free of tax and restrictions, and were not discriminated against in court. The Jewish religion was expressly approved and compulsory baptisms prohibited, as was any attempt to prevent the Jews from fulfilling their religious precepts. This peaceful phase, characterized by prosperity and inspiration, proceeded until the time of the Ottonians, although no evidence exists of continuous Jewish settlements until the 10th century in the German Empire. Jewish life is mentioned again for the first time in a document of Otto the Great from the year 965: "Judei et cetera mercatores," Jews and other merchants, are granted the privilege of trading in all wares and the permission to bring them into the country tax-free. This phrase made clear to what extent "Jews" and "merchants" had become synonymous. It expresses respect, referring as it does to the contribution Jewish merchants, traders and scholars made to the economic and social upswing, above all in the cities. Later, the bishop Rüdiger von Speyer, spiritual and secular lord of the city, paid them the same respect once again when he admitted that it was only the settlement of Jews that enabled a city to arise out of the "villa," the village Speyer.

The Jewish settlements and communities in the area comprising today's Germany came to be known collectively under the Biblical name of Ashkenaz. Ashkenaz was a descendent of the progenitor Noah, whose name was equated with the region "Germania." Its inhabitants, the Ashkenazim, differed from the Sephardim, who settled primarily in Spain in the trail of Islam, which had been pushing westwards from the 7th century on. Sepharad is the Biblical name for the Iberian peninsula where, for a long time, a second center of Jewish cultural life came into being and flourished until Jews were expelled from Spain at the end of the 15th century in the wake of the Christian reconquering and the Inquisition and were scattered in all directions once again—to Morocco, northern Italy, the Ottoman Empire and, from 1600 on, to the Netherlands, among other places.

right and opposite:
Jewish man and woman from Worms,
illustrations by Markus zum Lamm,
16th century
The bulb of garlic in his hands indicates
that the Jewish man is from Worms

underlay:
Eastern wall of the Speyer Synagogue,
built in 1104

Religious Life

Of the many cities in Ashkenaz in which a lively Jewish community life developed between the 10th and 13th centuries, the communities Speyer, Worms and Mainz—which developed into centers of cultural and spiritual life as well as Jewish scholarship—stand out. In these Schum communities—so called after the Hebrew initials of the place names and spelling out the Hebrew word for "garlic"—the foundation was laid for the tradition in Ashkenazic Judaism which has remained prominent to this day. And Germany's oldest synagogue, which had been in use for many centuries, was here in Worms, as well. One of the only things to remain intact following its destruction by the National Socialists in 1938 was the plaque of the donors Jakob ben David and his wife Rahel from the year 1034 (the synagogue was rebuilt in 1960 according to the old plans, but it remained insignificant as there was not a single Jewish family left in Worms).

Life in a Jewish community of the Middle Ages consisted of a communal baking oven to keep meals warm on the *Shabbat*, a cemetery, and often a "Heckhaus" or hospital and lodging for the poor and travelers. The plunge-bath or *mikveh,* often built deep into the earth, was used for ritual cleansing and served as a focal point for the women of the community. Dance halls were customary, as well, in which musicians would perform at community events. In the synagogue, however, music was not commonplace—here, thoughts should be directed towards the destruction of the temple. Soon various liturgies entered into the centers of Jewish life. Rabbi Jakob ben Moses of Mainz (1355–1427), called MaHaRiL, began to gather together customs and traditions developed over the course of centuries and to document their origin: did the symbolic ceremony at the time of the high religious holidays of casting sin into

The Erfurt Bible, ca. 1343

environment, Gershom created the basic structures for the Jewish communities which prevail to this day.

Gershom ben Jehuda became a spiritual forefather for many scholars, one of whom was the most important Ashkenazic Bible and Talmud expert of all: Rabbi Salomo ben Isaak (1040–1105), whose name was shortened to Rashi. His succinctly formulated commentaries on the Torah and the Talmud contributed to the spread and popularization of Talmudic knowledge. The religious legal decisions of the Ashkenazic rabbis in the Middle Ages were taken up in the 16th century into the standard work "Shulhan Arukh" or "The Prepared Table."

running water date back to a custom of the Christians of Cologne? Did the so-called *Yahrzeit*, commemorating a deceased person a year after his or her death, derive from a heathen custom?

The wealthy family Kalonymos, originally from northern Italy, played an essential role both in the community and the spiritual life of the time and in the foundation and differentiation of the Ashkenazic school. For generations, members of this influential and widely branched out family from Mainz acted as public representatives of the Jewish community, formed its economic backbone, and founded important Talmud academies, the *yeshivot*. The most important yeshivah in Mainz became the highest authority for central European Judaism in the 10th and 11th centuries. There, presumably appointed by the family Kalonymos, Rabbi Gershom ben Jehuda (960–1040) taught. He severed the Ashkenazic rabbis' dependence on the Babylonian and Palestinian religious schools and founded their independence. For this reason, he was posthumously honored with the title "Meor ha-Gola" or luminary in exile. His decisions and ordinances were recognized as binding all throughout western and central Europe. By trying to harmonize the religious fundaments of Judaism with the ethical and moral demands of a life in the midst of a Christian

The Crusaders

In Rashi's work, darker notes also resound: "We've had sad experiences in suffering and remain in constant danger of being destroyed." This was not a statement on events long since past, but rather on a catastrophe occurring before his very eyes. When Heinrich IV once again accorded the Jews of Worms

*View of the city of Worms, from the
Mogilev synagogue, Belarus, 18th century
above: Jewish musicians, illumination from 1471*

drive out the Muslim "infidels" and to reclaim the holy places, the animosity long suppressed broke out all the more fiercely: if Christ's enemies were to be fought in the Holy Land, then shouldn't they be fought all the more at home? Here, at least, rich booty could be had. Bands of crusaders came together spontaneously and without organization, and religious hatred and greed formed a murderous mixture among them. In the emperor's absence, who was in Italy at the time, and against the more or less vehement resistance on the part of local bishops and Christian citizens, the Jewish settlements on the Rhine were mercilessly overrun in the course of the year 1096. Hundreds of Jews in Speyer, Worms, Mainz, Trier, Metz, Cologne, Neuss, Xanten, or Regensburg were slain, burned, drowned, and the survivors given the ultimatum: baptism or death. In consequence, many chose to commit suicide as martyrs "to the sanctification of God," killing their children before taking their own lives. Whatever could be carried off of their victims' wealth the murderers divided among themselves.

When Heinrich IV, who condemned the massacre and threatened to call the criminals to account, returned in 1097 to Germany, he immediately renewed his old protection rights and allowed all those who had been forced into being baptized to convert back to Judaism. Although the Jewish communities recuperated, this attack on their very existence, without comparison in Europe up until that point in time, led to deep insecurity. The law had not been able to stand up to the rage of the mob. One result of the *pogroms* was a decentralization of Jews who until then had been living in a limited number of large cities and who were now increasingly settling in smaller towns. Another was a certain radicalness developing in a belief strengthened by martyrdom.

and Speyer extensive privileges in 1090, he placed them under his express protection "as belonging to the imperial chamber." The Jews' well-being rested nearly exclusively on their profitability for their rulers and was dependent among other things on the balance in power between emperor and pope, ruling princes and town councillors. Economic interests might have restrained the missionary and prophetic zeal among larger parts of the clergy for a long time, but by no means dissolved the antagonism between Christians and Jews.

When at the end of the Council of Clermont in November of 1095 Pope Urban II called upon the people and knights to travel to the Holy Land to

Thus, during the crusades, a special form of mysticism came into being whose members were called the Hasidim Ashkenaz, the "Pious of Germany." The founder of this school, which became influential in the 12th century, was Rabbi Jehuda ben Samuel (1170–1217), called Judah he-Hasid (the pious), a member of the Kalonymos family whose wife and two children had been murdered by crusaders. As a witness and victim of the cruelties of the crusades, Judah viewed world history as a self-sacrifice awaiting the arrival of the Messiah which can only be performed in firm loyalty towards God. Similar to the Spanish *kabbalists*, the "Pious of Ashkenaz" sought an emotional, personal, inner contact with God, and to this purpose recommended all kinds of magical practices and penitential exercises along with an ascetic and uncompromisingly devout way of life. Their elitist ideal was a community of saints who not only preserved the "old" faith to the letter, but at the same time recognized the spiritual and deeper hidden dimension of the Torah and Talmud. This Jewish mysticism made a deep impression on the religious culture of the Middle Ages.

The need for religious immersion also seemed to grow out of the increasing uncertainty and deteriorating legal situation. Undoubtedly with all good intentions, Heinrich IV placed Jews as "homines minus potentes" under his special protection in the "Mainzer Reichslandfrieden," an imperial prohibition of feuds; along with this, however, he took away their right to bear arms, which had a degrading effect in the long term.

Parallel to the religiously motivated polemics, attacks on the economic basis of the Jews were now occurring more and more frequently. The pawn-broking business increasingly lost ground due to the appearance of certificates of debt—or because in a

> "When a city has two synagogues, of which one is the closer and the other, farther away, is that frequented by the pious, it is better to go to the one that is farther away."
>
> JUDA HE-HASID

papal bull, Pope Eugenius III simply annulled the interest on credit the crusaders should have paid to their Jewish moneylenders. During the Fourth Lateran Council of 1215, led by Pope Innocent III, which aimed to create binding regulations for the relationship between Christians and Jews, new isolating measures were added, which were not, however, complied with everywhere. On the one hand, the limitation of interest on credit given by Jews was legitimized, and on the other, a "Kenn-

Alleged Theft of the Host from the Collegiate Church of the Cistercian cloister Heiligengrabe in Brandenburg, from a cycle of paintings, 1532

zeichnungspflicht" or obligation to mark oneself as a Jew was decreed: from now on, Jews had to wear the yellow patch of the proscribed on their clothing.

Church restrictions and the excesses against Jews on the other hand alarmed the secular powers, which saw their economic interests under attack. In order to lend their protection of the Jews new validity and to put an end to the Jews' legal uncertainty, Friedrich II introduced the legal system of the "Kammerknechtschaft" or a levied security for serfs. While this brought protection, it also put Jews entirely at the mercy of their lord's whim. If it pleased whomever they were subject to, or if it was of financial advantage to him, he could transfer the so-called Jewish prerogative to local rulers or cities. And a transferal of this kind took on an added attraction because the Kammerknechtschaft also resulted in the introduction of a regular poll tax.

The Black Death

From 1348, the plague heralded a new time of terror. The Black Death, imported by rats on ships from the Orient, decimated over a third of Europe's population. Because nobody could explain the reason for the deaths, rumors and speculations ran wild. And as so often before, Jews wound up at the center of suspicion. Already in the 13th century, Jews had been confronted continually with two types of defamation above all: on the one hand, they were accused of "Host sacrilege"—stealing the Host, perforating it and causing it to bleed. On the other, they were charged with "ritual murder"—wherever a child died inexplicably or disappeared, Jews were suspected of using the blood of Christian children to produce the unleavened bread for *Pessah*. Although these insinuations were condemned by the church, they often led to massacres of the Jewish population.

Now, at the height of the plague, Jews were held responsible for the inexplicable again and again: they were accused of poisoning the wells out of religious hatred and in revenge for the suffering imposed upon them, and causing the spread of the epidemic as a result. This led to bloody excesses which grew into systematic persecution. Thousands were murdered and the survivors driven out. By the end of 1350, nearly all German Jewish communities were destroyed. Even though many of those who fled

to the countryside returned after the end of the
plague and founded new communities, the experience of mass persecution was a crucial turning
point. Many survivors left the country, making for
northern Italy and Europe's eastern countries,
among other places. As a result, a significant Jewish
cultural life emerged, above all in Poland. The
emigrants took their language with them, the Jewish
German or West Yiddish, which consisted of Middle
High German dialects with Hebrew and Aramaic
elements. Gradually, with the addition of words bor-
rowed from the Slavic, Eastern Yiddish developed—
the language that soon became the lingua franca in
central eastern Europe and lives on to this day.

"Sefer Sinai" (The Book of Sinai)
by Abraham ben Baruch.
This manuscript from the late Middle
Ages (1391) is the oldest object in the
collection of the Jewish Museum Berlin

underlay:
The gravestone for "Jona, Son of Dan,"
erected in 1244, is the oldest documen-
tation of the Jewish Community in
Spandau

Shab

Penitential exercises being performed by Sabbatianists in Saloniki, engraving from Joseph Castein's book "Shabbtai Zvi. The Messiah of Ismir," Berlin, 1930

underlay: In "Yeven Mezulah" (Deepest Abyss), published in 1633, the contemporary chronicler Nathan Hannover describes the "unnatural horrors" that Cossacks inflicted on the Jews in Poland and the Ukraine

"And they did penance as never before, since the creation of the world ... At night the men lay down and rolled in the snow ... Then they took thorns and nettles and whipped themselves until their bodies were covered with blisters."

Leib ben Oser, the notary of the Ashkenaz community in Amsterdam, gave this impressive description of the unprecedented zeal to do penance that gripped Jews in Europe, North Africa and Asia Minor in 1665. In the fall of that year, reports had traveled from Palestine to all major cities that a man named Shabbtai Zvi had proclaimed himself the Messiah and had announced an imminent return to the Promised Land. Countless Jews, rich and poor, sold their possessions and prepared to follow Shabbtai Zvi. The shock was all the greater when the "Jewish Messiah" converted to Islam in 1666.

...tai Zvi—The False Messiah

The presumed Messiah Shabbtai Zvi and his prophet Nathan of Gaza, engravings from Thomas Coenens book "Ydele Verwachtinge der Joden," Amsterdam, 1669

Who was this man on whom the Jewish world pinned all its hopes in the 17th century?

Born in 1626 in Smyrna (today Izmir in Turkey), Shabbtai Zvi grew up studying the Talmud and Jewish mystical tradition known as the Kabbalah. Shabbtai was soon surrounded by a small group of followers who encouraged him in the belief that he had been chosen for a great cause. The special man wanted to do special things, and so quickly created enemies by violating religious laws. After the elders of Smyrna had expelled him from his community around 1654, he traveled for many years. In Gaza, he met the kabbalist Nathan, who had already seen a vision of the Redeemer in his youth. Nathan convinced Shabbtai that he, the banished man from Smyrna, was the Messiah. Innumerable circular letters spread the message with amazing success. In December 1665, Shabbtai Zvi set out to overthrow the Sultan and take over power. Jews throughout the world eagerly awaited news from Constantinople, but what began as a triumphal march ended in catastrophe. The authorities arrested Shabbtai Zvi and forced him to convert to Islam. He died in the remote fortress of Dulcigno in what is now Albania.

Why were so many Jewish communities caught up in the messianic frenzy surrounding Shabbtai Zvi?

Most Jews shared the yearning for release from their sufferings in the Diaspora. There were persecutions and expulsions everywhere: those who were not exposed to constant outbreaks of anti-Jewish violence such as the Jews in Germany learned through reports of the horrors experienced by Jews in many parts of the world. And it was precisely around the mid-17th century that these events reached a climax: the massacres carried out under the Cossack leader Bogdan Chmielnicki in 1648 virtually eliminated all Jewish life in eastern Europe. Even Glikl bas Judah Leib, the merchant living in Hamburg, felt the effects of the waves of persecution. In her memoirs, she recounts the fate of her relative, Abraham Hameln, who fled Poland and the violence of the Cossacks to reach northern Germany: "When... all Jewish communities and the whole of Poland were in great distress, he escaped with his wife and a daughter, naked and without a thing to their name, and came to my father-in-law." The tales of refugees such as Abraham Hameln evoked a basic feeling of insecurity and increased hopes of salvation—which were not, however, to be fulfilled through Shabbtai Zvi.

Hamburg Viewed from the Banks of the Elbe,
painting by Elias Galli, 1680

underlay: Memorial entry (Yizkor) for
Glikl bas Judah Leib upon her death in 1724
(on the left, center)

"The heavens had opened"

The Memoirs of Glikl bas Judah Leib

My dear children, I began writing this book with God's help after the death of your pious father to quiet my soul a bit when melancholy thoughts and worries weighed down on me." It was the year 1691 when the widowed merchant woman Glikl bas Judah Leib began writing down her memoirs—an extraordinary testimony to Jewish life on the threshold to a new century, a time of great change and upheaval.

The Thirty Years' War was drawing to a close when a daughter was born in 1646 to the elder of the Ashkenazic community of Hamburg, Judah Leib, and his wife Bele. She herself wrote her name Glikl bas Judah Leib, or Glikl, daughter of Judah Leib. Because she later married Chaim Goldschmidt of Hameln, she came to be known to literary posterity as "Glückel of Hameln."

תיקון קריאת
שמע

רבונו של עולם הריני מוחל לכל מי שהכעיס והקניט אותי
או שהטא כנגדי בגופי בממוני בין בכבודי · בין
בכל אשר לי בין באונס בין ברצון בין בשוגג בין במזיד בין בדבור
בין במעשה בין בגלגול זה בין בגלגול אחר לכל בר ישראל ולא יענש
שום אדם בסבתי ; יהי רצון מלפניך יי אוא שלא אחטא ומה · ש
שחטאתי מחוק ברחמיך הרבים ולא על יסורין ; יהיו לרצון אמרי
פי והגיון לבי לפניך יי צורי וגואלי ◊

*Woman at her Evening Prayers,
illumination by Aaron Wolf Herlingen,
Vienna, 1724*

In 1649, soon after the end of the war and in resistance to the economic competition of Jewish merchants, the Hamburg citizenry succeeded in expelling the Jews from the city to Altona, where the Danish king granted them protection, unlimited rights of residence, and freedom of religion. When Altona was captured by the Swedes, they were forced to return to Hamburg, where their existence remained constantly under threat. Jews were not granted permits of residence for the city, were compelled to hold prayer gatherings in "their secret, small, prayer houses," and had to reckon with renewed expulsion at any time.

Glikl's father traded primarily in jewels. He attained solid prosperity at this time of the absolutist princely courts with these luxury goods and his talent for business. His children were taught in the *heder,* the Jewish elementary school, where they learned reading and writing and received religious instruction. Glikl also received this basic education.

"By fretting over everything the way we do, we weaken our bodies, and with such careworn bodies we are unable to duly serve our Lord on high. For the divine Holy Spirit does not reside in a careworn body."

GLIKL BAS JUDAH LEIB

The Businesswoman

At the age of twelve, Glikl was betrothed to Chaim of Hameln, whom she married at fourteen. The couple set up house in Hamburg and Glikl gave birth to her daughter Zipora, the first of fourteen children. Chajim traded in gold and jewels, and Glikl not only managed the extensive household with its servants, private instructors, business assistants, and "Blettenjuden," Jews the community sent to them for food and lodging; at the same time, she was her husband's business partner, joining him on important business decisions and conducting contract negotiations as well as keeping the books.

It was not unusual for women to be active in trade. In Hamburg, women were allowed to set up business without the consent of their husbands from 1603 on. Glikl's grandmother had already lent money, and as a young woman her mother had run a workshop for gold and silver bobbin lace. Jewish as well as Christian widows frequently succeeded their husbands after their death in the businesses they were familiar with through the bookkeeping. In 1689, Chaim died after an accident, making his wife a widow at the age of forty-four. When asked about his will on his deathbed, he answered: "My wife, she knows everything. Let her do what she's been doing all along."

Glikl reorganized her life. She auctioned off the property to free herself of debts, founded a stocking manufactory, lent money and acquired an impeccable reputation as a successful and serious businesswoman. She was able to provide her children with sufficient dowries and to arrange good marriages for them. In her memoirs, she reminisces about her daughter Zipora's magnificent wedding to Elias Cleve from the Gomperz family, who belonged to the elite of the court Jews. The Great Elector sent his son to this wedding of "his Jews," where numerous "distinguished personalities" were present. The marrying of sons and daughters was regarded as an investment in the future—and not only for the business connections attached: having relatives in places that were comparatively secure for Jews often proved life-saving in times of danger.

Jewish merchants commonly used date tables such as this one, published by Judah ben Samuel Reutlingen Mehler in 1649 under the title "sefer ha-Evronot," to reconcile Christian market days with the Jewish calendar

Seven Books

From 1691 to 1719, Glikl filled a total of seven books with writing about her life and views. One of her sons later copied the originals—now lost without a trace—and thus passed them on to posterity. The memoirs and their significance were rediscovered in the 20th century by Bertha Pappenheim, founder of the Jewish Women's Association, who translated them into High German. These memoirs are considered to be the first written memories of a Jewish woman. Glikl had composed them in West Yiddish, her everyday language. Numerous quotations from the Bible and the Talmud indicate how well-read she was.

In her memoirs, Glikl looks back on her life as a successful businesswoman who as often as not carried jewels "worth thousands" in her pockets on her dangerous travels, who had to put up with adversity and need. She didn't want to write a "book of morals," she claimed, yet she gave advice for a "pious and God-fearing" life, observing the daily prayer times and reading regularly in the Torah. She wrote about her concerns for her family and children, reported of disputes within the community and of the false Messiah Shabbtai Zvi. Seized by a yearning for release from an environment hostile to Jews,

Glikl's parents-in-law, like many others, started preparing to return to the Holy Land: "Some people sold all their belongings. My father-in-law—may he rest in peace—lived in Hameln. So, he left everything behind … He sent two large barrels to us in Hamburg, filled with linens of every variety. And inside there was all sorts of food … for the good man—may he rest in peace—believed one would simply set off for the Holy Land from Hamburg."

Exhausted by the hardships of traveling as a merchant, Glikl bas Judah Leib wanted to retire from business at the age of fifty-five, but didn't want to become a burden to her children. After eleven years of being a widow, she married, with great hesitation, Hirsch Levy, the respected banker and head of the community in Metz. She gave her new husband her entire savings as a dowry. Two years later, his business went bankrupt and he died shortly thereafter. Now, what Glikl had always been afraid of had come to pass: she was forced to give up her independence and move into the home of her daughter. Later, she called her second marriage the biggest mistake of her life.

She died in 1724. Her entire life had been embedded in deep religious practice. Borne aloft by traditional Judaism, Glikl ultimately found comfort in the face of all of life's adversity. She wrote: "One must entrust everything to God, and know that this vain world shall soon have its end." Her last entry in the seventh book of her memoirs, dated 1719, describes how the clouds of the night sky break apart above the river Mosel, becoming for a moment as bright as day: "The heavens had opened, and afterwards the heavens closed again, as though someone had drawn a curtain shut, and it became very dark once again."

Bertha Pappenheim as Glikl,
portrait by Leopold Pilichowski, before 1925

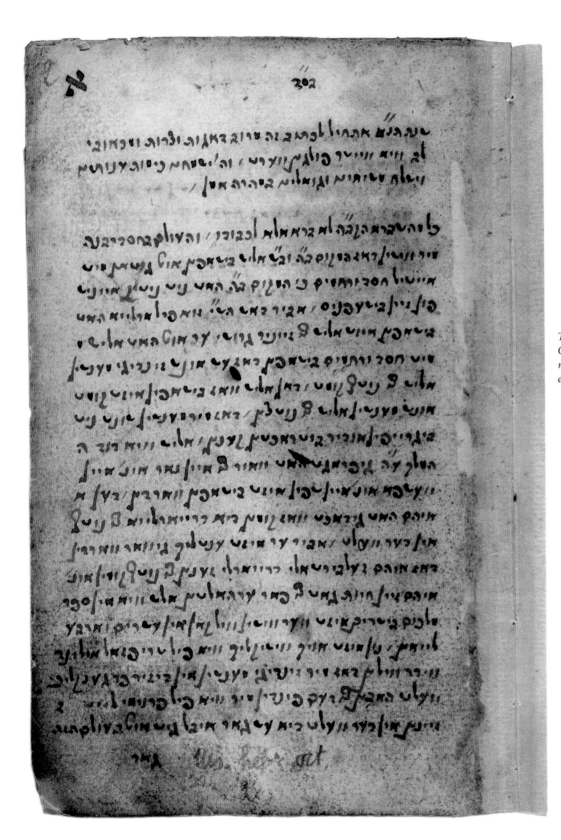

The opening of the memoirs of
Glikl bas Judah Leib in a copy
made by her son Moses Hamel,
early 18th century

Tradition and Change—
The Dietary Laws

What is Kosher?

The dietary laws are an example for how the Jewish religion penetrates every area of daily life; religious practice is not restricted to a certain time or location. The dietary laws are a part of the Halakhah, which also regulates the area of eating. This area and its precepts are called the *"Kashrut"* in their entirety. *Kosher* literally means pure, suitable, appropriate, and designates edibles that correspond to the rules and are permissible. Kitchen devices, tableware, and everything that has anything to do with the area of eating in the broadest sense can also be kosher or *trefe*, non-kosher.

There are foodstuffs that are essentially permitted or forbidden: animals living on land have to have cleft hooves and be ruminants (such as the cow and the lamb, but not the pig); sea animals have to have fins and scales; poultry is generally kosher with the exception of predatory birds. Warm-blooded animals must be killed according to Jewish rites, ritually slaughtered in the correct manner and prepared for consumption in a special way.

CONTENT: 1 KG.

KIDRON
WHITE
SUGAR

תכולה: 1 ק"ג

סוכר לבן
קידרון

Kosher sugar, Germany, 1998

*underlay: Kosher certificate for sugar,
Berlin, July 31, 2000*

Brass and steel slaughtering knife,
probably Germany, early 20th century

The Kosher Kitchen

"You should not cook the young goat in its mother's milk":
this proscription occurs three times in the Torah, from which
the rabbis derived the general prohibition against eating meat
and milk together. Fish, eggs, vegetables, fruit, and grains are
neutral, termed *parve*, and may be combined with both. For
religious Jews, the strict adherence to this commandment
means the consistent separation of all cooking utensils
coming into contact with milk and meat: dishes, cutlery, pots,
dishcloths, tablecloths, sinks, and, for some, refrigerators as
well. As do all other rules of religious law, the dietary laws
serve to sanctify daily life. The adherence to purity laws is a
prerequisite for communal meals, which frequently leads to a
separation between the private living areas of observant Jews
and non-Jews.

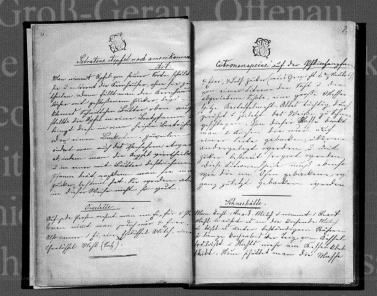

Notebook with recipes for kosher
dishes, Berlin 1884

Dishes differentiated by color
to ensure the separation of
dairy and meat products,
late 20th century

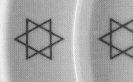

Vereinigung des
Marckt Fleckens
Ichenhausen von dem
Freyh: Sigmund vom
Stain an

Christians and Jews pay homage to the new lord
of the borough of Ichenhausen. In this painting from
1784, the Jewish population are depicted smaller
and at a greater distance from the lord's family

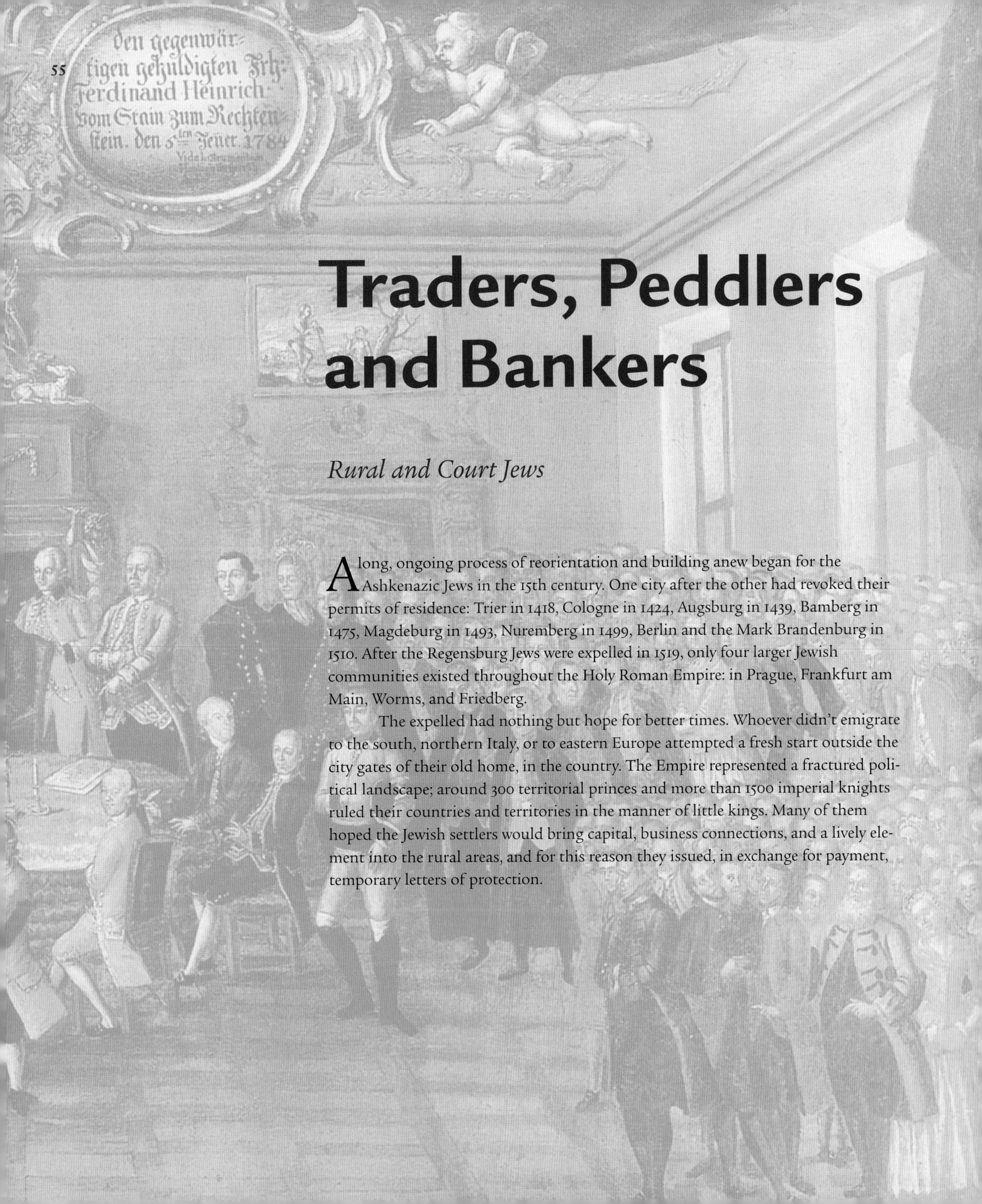

den gegenwär-
tigen gehuldigten Frh:
Ferdinand Heinrich
vom Stain zum Rechten
stein. den 5ten Feuer. 1784

Traders, Peddlers and Bankers

Rural and Court Jews

A long, ongoing process of reorientation and building anew began for the Ashkenazic Jews in the 15th century. One city after the other had revoked their permits of residence: Trier in 1418, Cologne in 1424, Augsburg in 1439, Bamberg in 1475, Magdeburg in 1493, Nuremberg in 1499, Berlin and the Mark Brandenburg in 1510. After the Regensburg Jews were expelled in 1519, only four larger Jewish communities existed throughout the Holy Roman Empire: in Prague, Frankfurt am Main, Worms, and Friedberg.

The expelled had nothing but hope for better times. Whoever didn't emigrate to the south, northern Italy, or to eastern Europe attempted a fresh start outside the city gates of their old home, in the country. The Empire represented a fractured political landscape; around 300 territorial princes and more than 1500 imperial knights ruled their countries and territories in the manner of little kings. Many of them hoped the Jewish settlers would bring capital, business connections, and a lively element into the rural areas, and for this reason they issued, in exchange for payment, temporary letters of protection.

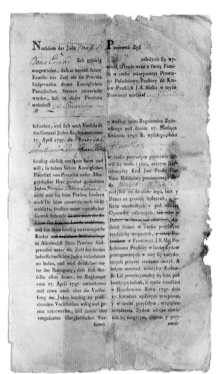

underlay: Letter of protection for the merchant Moses
Boas Eduard, Posen, dated October 20, 1798

Rural Jews

The Jews scattered throughout the south and west of
Germany had lost their social milieu and community support, and a Jewish family was often the
only one in a given location. Thus, in the absence of
daily fellowship in religious ceremony and common
prayer on the holy days in the country, they were all
the more dependent on the goodwill of their
Christian environment to continue pursuing their
religion. Furthermore, many of the professions they
had previously practiced were now barred to them.
They were admitted neither to state and military
service nor were they allowed to work as farmers or
craftsmen, and in many places the possession of
property was forbidden, as well. How, then, were they
supposed to eke out a living and pay the levies the
respective sovereigns were demanding of them?

The economic niche left to them was trade,
above all with rural goods such as horses, cattle,
grain and hops, and later tobacco—but also with city
products that were high in demand in the country
such as clothing, fabrics, and lengths of silk. Thus,
livestock trade and peddling developed into the
most important professional fields for the rural
Jews. In those days, being a peddler was by no means
dishonorable; peddlers were traveling salesmen, wandering merchants. They acquired wares in the cities
or from the farmers and sold them elsewhere or
traded them for natural produce. Heavily laden with
carrying gear, they roamed from village to village
throughout the week, returning home only on
Friday to spend Shabbat with their families. Their
wearisome activity was not only of central economic
significance to the rural population; at the same
time, it fulfilled an important social function. For
the Jewish peddlers also acted as "living newspapers"
who kept the farmers up to date on all the news and
gossip from the surrounding villages and cities. Even
into the 20th century, Jewish small traders contributed considerably towards the basic provision of
the rural regions.

Every form of trade is based on a balance of
interests. As with the peddlers and their regular
customers, communities of economic interests also
developed between the Christian farmers and Jewish
livestock dealers, for example with the so-called
"Viehverstellung" or cattle arrangement. Whoever
couldn't afford their own livestock, and many of the
smaller farmers couldn't, received a pregnant cow
"on deposit" that the farmer could use for working
the fields and whose milk and dung he was permitted to keep. In return, he fed the cow and raised the

"The Jews have maintained Shabbat and the Shabbat has sustained the Jews."

JEWISH PROVERB

calf. When a buyer for the animal was later found, the price was divided between the farmer and the dealer—a lucrative business low in risk for both sides.

Although everyday contact of this nature shaped the co-existence of Jews and Christians, the political situation remained precarious for the modestly earning rural Jews: their legal status was insecure and depended on the favor of the respective sovereign, which could be arbitrarily granted or revoked at any time, and Christian competition and the envy and ill will of neighbors could spontaneously switch over into hatred. In his diatribe "On the Jews and their Lies," published in 1543, the friar Martin Luther for example expressed the sentiment of his time and elevated anti-Judaism to an agenda: the synagogues were to be set on fire and the houses of the Jews destroyed; their holy books were to be taken away from them and, under threat of death, their rabbis forbidden to give any kind of lessons whatsoever; they were to be prohibited from every business activity and all their property was to be taken from them. The best thing would be to hunt them out of the land altogether.

Establishing a Jewish infrastructure proved to be exceedingly difficult under the circumstances, and most Jews had to manage without a resident rabbi and a cemetery of their own. It was often impossible to gather together a *minyan*—the ten men of age whose presence was required before worship could take place. Thus, the family, a talent for improvisation, and piousness came to form the back-

bone of Judaism. Prayer halls were built and decorated wherever people couldn't afford a synagogue; the rabbi from the nearest rabbinate was only called in for advice in the most urgent cases; and the dead sometimes had to be transported across many borders to be buried in consecrated earth, incurring high costs in customs fees. And, as is often the case in dire times, when evil powers are suspected of being at work, mysticism and a belief in spirits was on the rise.

Detail from the ceiling of a Jewish prayer room in Unterlimpurg (Schwäbisch Hall), 1735–36, showing the Biblical creature Leviathan

"Jewish Alleys" and "Jewish Quarters"

This was a situation in which external circumstances opened up unexpected perspectives to Jews. The absolutist state that was developing with an increasingly economically orientated concept of rule took care to tax every subject according to his or her usefulness. It charged the Jews protection and head levies, taxes on wares and "gifts." As a special duty, a sovereign may demand the tongue of every slaughtered animal.

Each individual territory was now setting up its own central structures, which allowed Jews to establish unified territorial committees and to employ state rabbis. Thus, from the second half of the 16th century on, "Landjudenschaften" were formed that became the new institution of self-administration among Jews in the German states. Even the Thirty Years' War, which laid waste to the continent from 1618, provided opportunities for those merchants considered indispensable as financiers or military suppliers for the various warring parties. Under the protection of the Catholic Imperial Habsburg troops, many of those once expelled returned, reinforcing both the Jewish communities that had survived and those that were in the process of establishing themselves anew.

Jews were now settling again in the cities, such as Heidelberg, Mannheim, Hamburg, Osnabrück, and Münster, in spite of the vehement protests of Christian state administrations, mayors, and guilds. Thus, "Jewish quarters" with public synagogues and

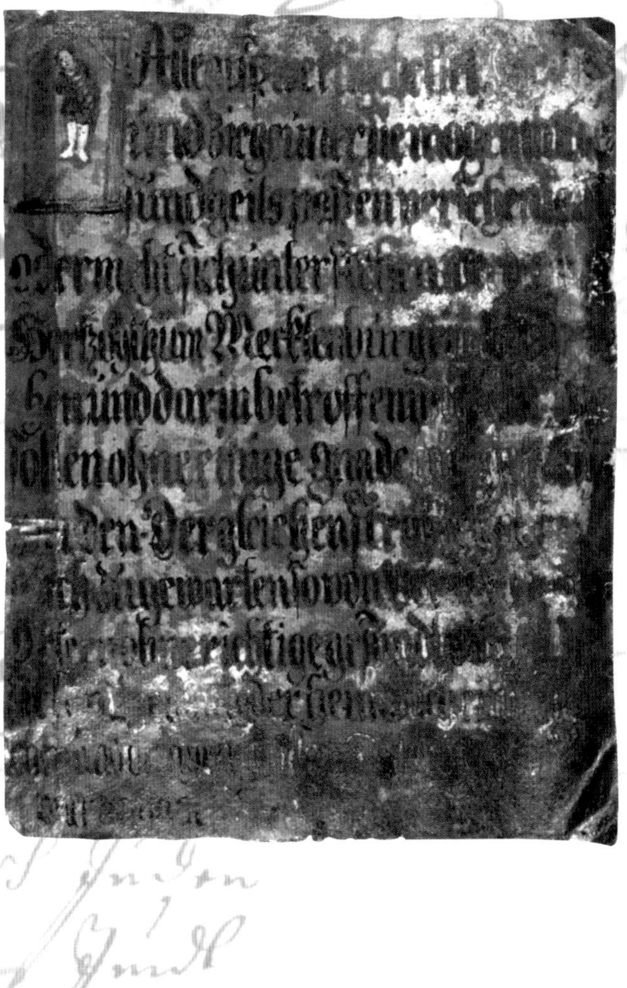

Warning sign for Jewish beggars and "gypsies" in Mecklenburg, ca. 1750

underlay: Poll tax receipts stamped with grimacing faces

"Jewish alleys" in the smaller villages came into being and often constituted the center for trade. Although strong forces attempted to reverse this development after the war ended in 1648—indeed resulting in renewed expulsions, for instance in Lübeck, Augsburg, and Schweinfurt—the majority of the territorial rulers adhered instead to a new political virtue coming to the fore, the raison d'état.

Yet, as much as the new state pragmatism on the one hand meant progress and the reanimation of Jewish life in Germany, on the other it exacerbated social polarization. Only a minority was wealthy enough to afford the pleasures of the privileges being offered. Whoever applied for a letter of protection had to reveal his financial circumstances in painstaking detail. In Prussia, an applicant was normally only accepted if he was in possession of more than 1,000 thalers. Thus, for example, the Great Elector Friedrich Wilhelm of Brandenburg signed an edict of settlement for fifty Jewish families in May of 1671, "as long as they are rich and wealthy people who want to bring their means into the land and invest it here"—150 years previously, Jews had been expelled from Brandenburg "for eternity." Regulations such as these, which helped the absolutist sovereigns keep the number of their Jewish subjects as low as possible while deriving a maximum in profit, resulted in thousands of Jews becoming reduced to beggarly vagabonds throughout the 17th century. Since the state refused "Jewish beggars" permits of residence and domicile, they were forced to wander through the rural areas, subsisting on their right to charity. For to help the poor is a mitzvah, a central religious commandment. No one without a letter of protection was permitted to remain in a location for more than one night. Thus, the Jewish communities handed out "Bletten" or coupons for a night's stay and a meal with a Jewish family.

In the long run, it proved impossible to counteract the spread of poverty with charity and solidarity alone. In order to create a better forum for Jewish interests, a stronger political influence was required. In this respect, the small wealthy class took on a special role. A new leading elite arose at their head towards the end of the 17th century: the court Jews, who were now to a greater extent continuing what their predecessors had begun during the Thirty Years' War.

Two Beggars,
etching by Jakob Steinhardt,
1909

Court Jews

The German sovereigns of the 17th and 18th centuries looked on in envy and admiration at the French court and the way in which French sovereignty, hemmed in neither by the landed aristocracy nor by the provincial legislatures, put itself on display with its magnificent palaces and military splendor. France became a model, yet in order to imitate it, considerable financial means were necessary which could not be amassed through the traditional manner of taxation, as long as the right to approve a tax remained in the hands of the respective provincial legislatures and not the sovereign. The only possibility to compete with the French model without having to seek the representatives' agreement for every larger expenditure was to procure credit. And to this purpose, the sovereigns now made frequent use of the know-how and experience of those Jews who had specialized in matters of money and credit and had contacts to the European financial centers at their disposal—in particular Amsterdam, Vienna, London, and Paris. Before long, there was hardly a German sovereign who believed he could get by without the services of a court Jew. The court Jew received status and title, was thenceforth permitted to call himself court factor, court agent or financial counselor, was freed of all degrading special levies, and was able to enjoy the privileges of a member of court.

The small group of court Jews acquired an increasing sense of elitism and considered themselves part of the European ruling class—their descendants were often active well into the 19th century as private bankers. Although some members of this upper stratum converted to Christianity, the majority remained rooted in Jewish tradition and were actively involved in their communities. Like Samuel Oppenheimer (1630–1703), they used their strong position at court to improve the legal, social, and economic situation of their fellow Jews. In doing so, they were treading a fine line. Permanently dependent on the good will and support of their sovereigns, they were at the mercy of their princely moods: if it occurred to the sovereign, he could just as easily cross out millions in received loans with the stroke of a pen, leaving his court Jew in the lurch to face the creditors alone.

The court Jews often also took the blame for unpopular measures. One of the business sectors they looked after, for example, was the coinage system, from the procurement of precious metals to their mintage into money. In times of emergency, however, instances of decreed coinage fraud or so-called coin deterioration occurred repeatedly. When the state coffers were nearly emptied during the Seven Years' War (1756–1763), for example, and Frederick the Great was afraid he could no longer finance his military campaigns, he commissioned his coin agent, Veitel Heine Ephraim (1703–1775), to recoin the one-third thaler, reducing the amount of silver while retaining the same denomination. People were outraged, but instead of holding their king accountable for the deception, they blamed his court Jew: "On the outside silver, on the inside tin / On the outside Frederick, on the inside Ephraim" was a popular saying of the time.

far left: Iud Ioseph Süs Oppenheimer, Former Financial Advisor, copper engraving by an anonymous artist, Stuttgart, February 4, 1738

left: Jud Süss Oppenheimer in Custody and at the Announcement of the Verdict, copper engraving by Elias Baeck, alias Heldenmuth, Augsburg, 1738

To what extent the court Jews were performing on the edge of a deep abyss is proven in an exemplary way by the fall of Joseph Süss Oppenheimer, whose story already polarized people in his own time. During the National Socialist regime, propaganda minister Goebbels saw to it that Oppenheimer was stylized into the demonic Jew par excellence, acquiring a new and sad fame in the anti-Semitic agitation film "Jud Süss" by Veit Harlan.

Oppenheimer first came to be called "Jud Süss" on the day of his arrest in 1737. Born in 1698, his rise to banker, financial counselor of Württemberg, and close advisor to the Duke Carl Alexander portrays the precarious and dangerous situation court Jews inevitably found themselves in during the time of small state absolutism. Oppenheimer modernized Württemberg's financial system, did away with the old privileges of the representatives and reformed the state budget; yet with each growth in the state finances, the number of the envious and antagonistic increased. When the Duke died unexpectedly in 1737, Oppenheimer fell prey to the revenge of his enemies. He was arrested and, following a questionable trial that was quickly hatched, badly prepared, and always on the verge of an open judiciary scandal, sentenced to death. It was impossible to prove that he committed a fiscal or political crime, yet in the eyes of his accusers, the "lecherous seducer," the "cold-blooded businessman," the "free thinker," and "Jew" deserved to hang. On the morning of February 4, 1738, Joseph Oppenheimer died on the highest gallows of the empire. The more than 12,000 spectators present, more than half of Stuttgart's population, turned his execution into a macabre feast. His body was hung in a cage and put on display for six days outside the city gates, visible from afar.

Despite such bitter setbacks, Jewish life in Germany had gained in stability. The size and number of the Jewish communities increased. Due to persistent restrictions and an agricultural crisis, however, this increase became a problem during the first half of the 19th century. The demographic pressure, above all on the rural Jews from southern Germany, became stronger and stronger. Their situation worsened to such a degree that many rural dwellers fled to the cities. Through the liberties fought for and achieved in the 1860s, Jewish merchants could now at last move to cities and small market towns on the railroad lines and establish permanent shops. A prominent example of this rural flight is Adolf Jandorf, the founder of the legendary department store "Kaufhaus des Westens" in Berlin. Jandorf always maintained ties to his home town of Hengstfeld in Württemberg—he supported the fire brigade, sponsored a war memorial, and was made an honorary citizen. Hundreds of thousands of country dwellers were also lured to the New World, just like that young man from Bavarian Franconia who boarded a steamship as Löb Strauss in 1847 and who was destined to make a career in New York—from where his "waist overalls," better known as Levi Strauss' blue jeans, conquered the world.

Copy of the Illustrierter Film-Kurier, with the poster for the film "Jud Süss" on the cover, 1940

right: Käthi Frenkel-Bloch with berhes

below: Synagogue of the rural community
of Endingen in Switzerland, 1987

underlay: The cattle market outside of Buttstädt in
Thuringia, copper engraving by Christian Richter, 1650

Nowadays, such dishes as gefilte fish, bagels and falafel are well-known examples of Jewish cooking. They each have a history of their own, however, and the recipes are closely related to their regions of origin. Gefilte fish is a typical dish of eastern Europe, while in southern Germany rural Jews ate fish garnished with "green sauce" rich in herbs, which originated in Frankfurt. Of course, in their cooking the rural Jews used the ingredients common to the regions where they lived and adapted existing local recipes to their own kashrut laws. It is very likely that at some time in the Middle Ages the dumplings still popular in southern Germany, Austria, and Bohemia inspired the Jewish *mazzah* balls prepared at Pessah.

Rural Jewish specialities of southern Germany

Rural Jews, especially the peddlers and livestock traders, had to cover great distances on foot to reach their regular customers' farms or the market towns.

In Christian inns, Jews were only allowed to drink beer and liquor, but not wine, as this had to be produced under Jewish supervision. Boiled eggs and raw vegetables were the only foods they were permitted to eat. So, on their travels, they had to either take along kosher dishes or prepare them themselves. On Shabbat, rural Jews normally ate food rich in calories, such as *berhes or hallah*, the braided bread traditionally baked on Friday afternoon. This type of bread still survives, especially in towns and villages where there were once Jewish communities, but its origin is often forgotten.

The continuing tradition

Even after rural Jews resettled in towns and cities, Jewish housewives continued preparing the traditional regional dishes. This helped to create a sense of family cohesion, especially on Jewish holidays.

In Switzerland, elements of rural Jewish culture have survived for a remarkably long time. Käthi Frenkel-Bloch from Dättwil has collected old rural recipes passed along in her family.

Rural Jewish Cooking

Berhes
900 grams (2 ¹/2 pounds) wheat flour
40 grams   yeast (1 cube or 1.4 ounces)
¹/2   deciliter (3 tablespoons) of oil
approx. 6 deciliter (2 ¹/2 cups) of warm water

Make the dough. Add the water slowly as the dough should not be too sticky. The quantity of water needed may vary. Allow the dough to rise in a warm place for about 2 hours, then cut into 3 or 4 pieces and braid the berhes. Leave to rise again for about 10 minutes. Brush with egg yolk, sprinkle with poppy seed and bake for about 45 minutes.

Mazzah Balls or Dumplings
2   egg yolks
2   egg whites
1   tablespoon chicken drippings
1   cup mazzah flour (or finely ground mazzah)
1   teaspoon salt
1   teaspoon ground ginger
¹/2 cup chicken stock

Mix together the flour, salt, and ginger. Whisk the egg yolks with the lukewarm chicken drippings, then add the stock. Mix well. Beat the egg whites until stiff and fold in, then leave the dough for 1 hour in a cool place.

With wet hands, shape round walnut-sized dumplings, and simmer in ¹/2 liter pre-heated salted water for about 25 minutes in a covered pan. The mazzah balls can be served in chicken or beef stock or as a side dish.

All recipes are taken from Käthi Frenkel-Bloch's cook book "Achile heisst Essen," Baden, Switzerland: 1995.

Moses Mendelssohn,
portrait by August Theodor Kaselowsky
after AntonGraff, ca. 1855

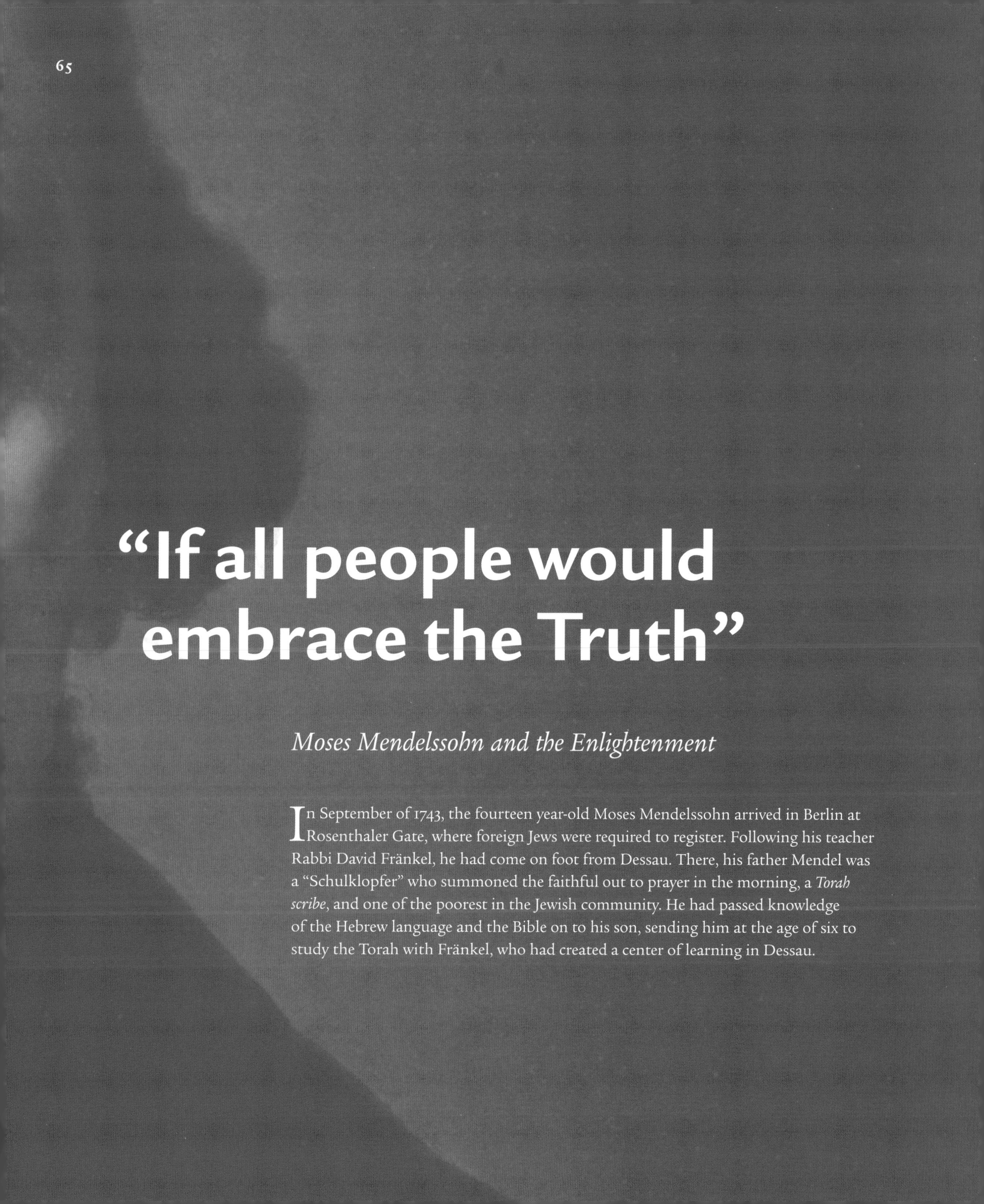

"If all people would embrace the Truth"

Moses Mendelssohn and the Enlightenment

In September of 1743, the fourteen year-old Moses Mendelssohn arrived in Berlin at Rosenthaler Gate, where foreign Jews were required to register. Following his teacher Rabbi David Fränkel, he had come on foot from Dessau. There, his father Mendel was a "Schulklopfer" who summoned the faithful out to prayer in the morning, a *Torah scribe*, and one of the poorest in the Jewish community. He had passed knowledge of the Hebrew language and the Bible on to his son, sending him at the age of six to study the Torah with Fränkel, who had created a center of learning in Dessau.

above and opposite:
Prussian edicts concerning peddlers,
money-changers, vagabonds,
and "gypsies" from the 18th century

In 1740, a new king stepped onto the throne in Prussia: Frederick the Great, the "philosopher king," who exhibited an openness for the ideas of the Enlightenment. Approximately 3000 Jews lived in Berlin, most of whom were poor. A few wealthy entrepreneurs who had profited from Frederick's mercantile economic policy were on more or less even footing with the Christian traders. Frederick granted the so-called "generally privileged" residence for dealing in "trade, commerce, manufacturing, factories, and the like." All other Jews were subject to strict regimentation—their permission of residence was limited, they were oppressed by special levies, and were only allowed to practice certain professions. "Worthy of a cannibal" was the judgment the French Count Mirabeau passed on laws of this kind.

The Haskalah

Fränkel, who arranged for Moses to stay in the house of the community's eldest, helped the poor Talmud student procure a residence permit. He just about managed to get by during the first years in Berlin—often on an empty stomach, in spite of the "Freitische" or free meals which Fränkel took care to provide him with. Mendelssohn had come to Berlin to study, and he was lucky with his teachers and friends. He acquired a "taste for the sciences" from Aaron Salomon Gumpertz (1723–1769), a doctor, mathematician and philosopher who kept in lively contact with various scientists and artists; from the Polish Talmud scholar Israel Samocz (ca. 1700–1772), he received instruction in mathematics, philosophy and literature.

Mendelssohn's teachers stood for a Jewish education open to secular knowledge, which marked the beginning of the inner-Jewish Enlightenment, the *Haskalah*. It initiated a process of reform that, in the 19th century, fundamentally changed the community, education, religious service, and ritual laws of Judaism. Mendelssohn, who belonged to the young generation of enlightened *Maskilim*, retained this belief in the necessity of studying non-Jewish works throughout his life: "The accusation of sectarianism doesn't frighten me out of taking from others with a grateful heart whatever I might find of use in their thought." He read the works of Locke and Hume, Leibniz' "Theodizee," the rationalist metaphysics of Wolff, and the works of the French Enlightenment.

The silk manufacturer Isaak Bernhard employed Mendelssohn as a private teacher. He worked six hours a day, and "all the remaining hours are left for me." Because he was one of the unprotected foreign Jews who were only tolerated as long as the Jewish community continued giving them food and lodging, Mendelssohn could have been expelled after his pupils grew up. It was only years later, when he had already long since become well-known outside Prussia's borders, that the king granted him the right of permanent residence. Bernhard made him bookkeeper and later business director and partner of his factory. After his death, Moses took over the direction of the firm and expanded it successfully.

The "Republic of the Learned"

Under the Prussian kings, the capital Berlin underwent an unprecedented boom. The population doubled within half a century to 100,000 inhabitants. Trade and manufacturing flourished. The Royal Academy of Sciences became a focal point for Europe's intellectual elite. Berlin, a city of the fine arts and a "republic of the learned," became a meeting place for enlightened Jewish intellectuals.

From 1748, a young man of the same age as Moses Mendelssohn had been living in the city, earning his living with newspaper work for the publisher Friedrich Nicolai: Gotthold Ephraim Lessing (1729–1781). When Gumpertz introduced him to Mendelssohn, Lessing met his ideal of an enlightened Jew, whom he immortalized in his play "Nathan the Wise." Their friendship was to last a lifetime. Mendelssohn enjoyed an inspired exchange of ideas with Lessing on questions of language and morals, art and aesthetics that had a crucial influence on his conception of the world. Twenty years later, Mendelssohn wrote an obituary for the man who "educated my soul," "whom I shall imagine as a friend and judge with every act I've planned, with every line I should write."

Through Lessing, Mendelssohn got to know the book

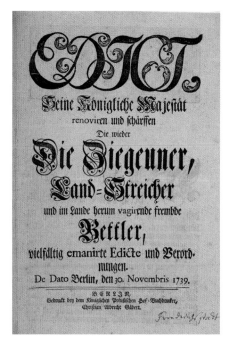

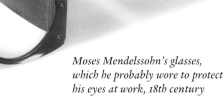

Moses Mendelssohn's glasses, which he probably wore to protect his eyes at work, 18th century

trader's son Friedrich Nicolai, who later became a famous Berlin publisher. Nicolai, publisher of the "Library of the Sciences and the Fine Arts" and the "Literature Letters," made Mendelssohn a co-worker. Nicolai later wrote to Lessing that he never left Mendelssohn "without having become either better or more learned." For the Christian businessman Nicolai, life was good in Frederick the Great's Berlin. When Lessing attacked Berlin as the "most slavish land in Europe," Nicolai responded that he could "do without" political freedom in a monarchistic country: "I can be silent." Just how different life was for the Jews, however, subject to a king who set such great store by his own tolerance and open-mindedness, but who in practice held on to a policy of patronizing, Moses recorded in sad words: "Here in this so-called tolerant country, I nevertheless live so restrictedly, so hemmed in on all sides by true intolerance that I have to lock myself up in a silk factory the whole day for the sake of my children. Now and again I go for a walk in the evening with my wife and children. Papa!, asks innocence itself, What is that fellow there calling after us? Why are they throwing stones at us? What did we do to them?—Yes, dear Papa!, says another, They always follow us in the streets and curse: Jews! Jews! Do they think that being a Jew is such a curse? And what stops others from doing the same? Alas! I cast down my eyes and sigh to myself: Humans! Humans! How far have you let things come?"

The Private Man and the Philosopher

Moses Mendelssohn married late. He left Berlin for the first time in 1761 and traveled to Hamburg. Four weeks later, he returned, in love. Lessing was the first to find out: "I have committed the foolishness of falling in love in my thirtieth year. You're laughing?... The woman I choose to marry possesses no fortune, she is neither beautiful nor learned, and nevertheless I, amorous fop, am so taken by her that I believe I will be able to live happily with her." Letters to Moses arrived twice a week from the twenty-four year-old Fromet, daughter of the optician Abraham Gugenheim. Fromet (1737–1812) carefully saved Moses' betrothal letters, and a great number of them have survived, telling us a lot about his everyday life. Of Fromet's life, however, we know nearly nothing.

Fromet and Moses were unusual people. They married without a marriage broker or *shadhan*. On the subject of the traditional marriage contract, Mendelssohn said: "Why make a pleasant duty into a compulsion?... Should I always consult the marriage contract any time I wish to do my wife a favor...?" Over the course of two decades, Fromet brought ten children into the world—three girls, Brendel, Recha, and Henriette, and three boys, Joseph, Abraham, and Nathan survived.

Since his days as a bookkeeper, Mendelssohn led a double life. He sat at his desk in the office until the early hours of the afternoon with "annoying business" which, he complained to Lessing, was

Moses Mendelssohn and his wife Fromet Gugenheim donated this Torah ark curtain, presumably made from Fromet's wedding dress, to a Berlin synagogue, dated 1774–75

draining the energy from his best years. Afterwards, he dedicated himself to writing, translating, and the study of philosophy. He regarded metaphysics as the queen of the sciences, as he had read at the age of twelve in the "More Newuchim" (Guide of the Indecisive), written by the medieval Spanish doctor and philosopher Moses Maimonides (1135-1204): "Know now, my son, that you, as long as you are involved with the mathematical sciences and logic, belong to those who walk around the house looking for the door. When you understand the natural sciences, however, you've already entered the courtyard, and when you've completed these entirely and direct your attention to metaphysics, then you have entered the house of the king." For the rest of his life, Mendelssohn regarded Maimonides as his spiritual mentor.

Mendelssohn earned public recognition for his writings on philosophy, literature, and aesthetics. In 1763, he won the first prize of the Royal Academy of Sciences for his treatise "On Evidence in the Metaphysical Sciences." The second prize was awarded to a private instructor from Königsberg: Immanuel

Kant. When, however, the Royal Academy elected Mendelssohn as a regular member, Frederick II refused to confirm the vote, holding on to his preconception that the state and its institutions had to be protected from the "destructive" influence of the Jews. The "Jew Moses," prizewinner of the Academy and long since celebrated as the leading thinker of the German Enlightenment, never became a member of the Academy.

With "Phaedo or On the Immortality of the Soul," which Nicolai published in 1767, Mendelssohn's reputation extended far beyond the borders of the city. In the form of a Socratic dialogue, he attempted to provide proof that a reasonable religion and the doctrine of immortality were "accessible and illuminating to the unspoiled human reason" and had only been obscured by "superstition, clerical cunning, the spirit of contradiction, and sophistry." Both Jews and Christians identified with "Phaedo." The book, translated into many languages, became one of the biggest bestsellers of its time, founding Mendelssohn's fame as "the philosophic writer of our nation" (Herder) and turning him into a European celebrity.

Both Worlds

Jews and non-Jews alike came to his house, writers, doctors, and free thinkers who debated the news of the day and discussed art and philosophy, books and theater performances. Women were only involved at the fringes. And yet, it was the daughters of Jewish fathers and mothers who continued this tradition of discussion in their salons—Rahel Varnhagen, Henriette Herz, and also Moses' daughter Brendel, better known to posterity as Dorothea Schlegel (1772-1839). Mendelssohn the enlightener attempted to unite the best of both worlds, the Jewish and the Christian, into a synthesis. He demanded tolerance of the Christians, and from Jews he demanded they shake off the isolation they had chosen for themselves. They should follow the religious law and

five books of Moses into German and had them set in Hebrew letters to remain accessible to Jews. With this, he met with categorical refusal among the Orthodox, who considered it a danger to the respect for tradition and the authority of the Talmud.

Just as heavily criticized was the establishment of schools by the Maskilim as part of their attempt to reform education, which they considered as being inseparably connected to the goal of "civil improvement." Mendelssohn supported the project of a first German Jewish "Freyschule" or free school, which was financed by the Berlin merchant Isaac Daniel Itzig (1750-1806) and was held in high regard, especially in its early years. Here, Jewish boys predominantly from poor families received instruction for the first time—from Christian as well as Jewish teachers—in German, arithmetic, writing, drawing, French, and bookkeeping, and were thus exposed to entirely different material than in a traditional Jewish lesson where the Torah and the Talmud were the central focus. David Friedländer (1750-1834), friend and pupil of Moses and the first Jew to enter the Berlin city council, designed the institution's program and curriculum, which focused on commercial knowledge. Together with Mendelssohn, he created a reader which was the first German-language book conceived for a Jewish school.

The enlighteners reaped criticism for the acculturation process they had introduced. Rahel

become loyal Prussian citizens, retain pride in their old culture while opening themselves up to the German: "Enter into the customs and constitution of the country you've been transplanted into; but keep true to the religion of your fathers. Carry both burdens as well as you can!" When the Swiss pastor Johann Caspar Lavater called upon him in 1769 to either refute Christianity or to let himself be baptized, Mendelssohn replied: "I hereby testify in front of the God of truth, your Creator and Keeper and mine... that I will stand by my principles, as long as my soul does not adopt another nature."

For his part, Mendelssohn succeeded in creating this synthesis: he was both an enlightened thinker and a devout Jew who spoke and wrote in German. In 1780—together with Solomon Dubno (1738-1813), Naftali Herz Wessely (1725-1805), and Herz Homberg (1749-1841), who with David Friedländer, Aaron Wolfssohn, and Lazarus Bendavid belonged to the leading minds of the Berlin Haskalah—he completed a translation of the

right and opposite:
This tea cup, made by the
Royal Porcelain Factory Berlin,
shows a portrait of the
"Royal Master Surveyor,"
Isaac Daniel Itzig;
the estate in Schöneberg,
which he acquired in 1786,
is depicted on the saucer

above:
Lavater and Lessing with
Mendelssohn—this lithograph,
after the painting by
Moritz Daniel Oppenheim,
portrays a fictional meeting.
In fact, the debate took place
by correspondence.
Paris, ca. 1856

Varnhagen found these contradictions to be fierce: "I have a fantasy; it's as though, while I was being pushed into this world, an other-worldly being had stabbed these words into my heart with a dagger while entering: 'Yes, have feelings, see the world as few see it, be great and pure … one thing was forgotten, though: be a Jew!', and now, my whole life, one long bleeding … every movement to stop it a new death." David Friedländer responded to a friend: "You want to send your son to Berlin, where in the morning he should spend a nice half day with Reb Meier ben Simche or some other such teacher, and in

Certificate of Naturalization granted to "the local banker Daniel Itzig and his legitimate descendants of both sexes." Berlin, May 2, 1791

opposite: David Friedländer, Portrait by Friedrich Georg Weitsch, ca. 1810

"Or is a woman's constitution conclusive evidence that she cannot think and cannot express her thoughts? Even were this so, she would still have the duty, or at least the right, to keep trying over and over again."

RAHEL VARNHAGEN

The ichthyologist and doctor Marcus Elieser Bloch (1723–1799), portrait by Johann Christoph Frisch, 1779

right: Red Gurnard, Trigla hirundo linnaeus, 1758, taxidermal mounting from the collection of Marcus Elieser Bloch

the afternoon he should be in a Christian school? That doesn't work. An entirely different human being is raised in each of these institutions. In the morning, one is supposed to place him in a world where everything looks different than in the real one he lives in, where people speak differently, act differently, discuss differently, and involve themselves with entirely different things than in the world of the afternoon…"

Moses Mendelssohn, however, never tired of fighting for his idea of tolerance: "What a happy world we would be living in if all people would embrace and practice the Truth the best Christians and the best Jews have in common." His intellectual legacy on this question and perhaps his most important book is "Jerusalem or On Religious Power and Judaism" of 1783. No religion can claim absolute truth. Tolerance is the highest duty of all. Church and state must be strictly separated. Just as the state has no right to impose faith or to deny someone his civil rights because of his religious persuasion, the church should also not be allowed to exercise force and compulsion over opinion. "Jerusalem" was a defense of his double intellectual connection: a plea for reason against the power of dogma, but also for the law that God had given his people on Mount Sinai.

On the morning of January 4, 1786, Moses Mendelssohn died at the age of fifty-seven, three years before the French Revolution. On the day of his burial, all Jewish shops and offices were closed. Jewish Berlin mourned the philanthropist and servant of an enlightened reason who had lived for his dream of a tolerant and equal relationship between Jews and Christians.

Tea and Talk— The Berlin Salons

Around 1800, the so-called salons developed in Berlin. Jews and Christians, women and men, aristocrats and commoners met here and debated current affairs, literature, art, and politics. The hostesses of these meetings between writers, leading civil servants, actors, and members of many different professions were frequently the educated Jewish women of Berlin. In the flourishing bourgeois society, education was seen as the key to a moral way of life, social rise, and equality in civil rights. Social contacts between Jews and non-Jews were fairly rare in those days, so the salons provided new openings for educated people to interact.

Henriette Herz as Hebe, the Greek goddess of youth, portrait by Anna Dorothea Therbusch, 1778

The first salon of this kind was established by Henriette Herz (1764–1847), the young wife of the physician and philosopher Marcus Herz (1747–1803). Henriette was bored by the regular lecture evenings that Marcus held in their apartment on topics related to philosophy and physics. She was more interested in contemporary literature, and soon began inviting people to her own evening discussions. And so, for a time, two different groups met at the Herz': the older generation that was decidedly in favor of strict reasoning, and the younger people, who gathered for lively readings and discussions on the new Romantic literature—the salon. The Herz salon in Berlin also greatly encouraged the growing appreciation of Goethe, which occasionally slipped into gushing enthusiasm, especially among the young women.

Rahel Levin was born in 1771 as the eldest daughter of the jeweler Markus Levin. Although Rahel considered herself not educated enough, she spoke both German and French, could write in Hebrew script and began reading contemporary literature and philosophy as a young girl. Rahel was the first unmarried woman to cultivate her own salon. She began her gatherings after her father's death in 1790; her attic apartment became an important focal point for Berlin's educated circles. However, the war with France temporarily put an end to this salon in 1806. In 1814, Rahel married the diplomat Karl August Varnhagen von Ense. She lived with him in a number of different places. When they returned to Berlin five years later, a salon gathered around Rahel again, which soon became a fashionable Berlin institution.

However, the salons of Henriette Herz and Rahel Varnhagen were not the only ones of this kind. Others were established, for instance by Sara von Grotthuss (1763–1828) or the banker's widow Sara Levy (1761–1854). The regular encounters in Sara Levy's salon centered around music, and she promoted the music of the Bach family with great fervor. Other musical salons took place at the homes of the Beers and the Mendelssohn-Bartholdys.

The fall of Napoleon in 1813 and the subsequent Restoration era brought a change in the social climate, and anti-Jewish prejudices increased. Attacks were leveled against educated Jews in particular, including the women and their salons. Christian patriotism was the slogan of the day and many of their former guests turned towards such ideas. The era of the salon came to an end.

Declaration of the Rights of Man and the Citizen, France 1789

underlay: View of the Brandenburg Gate and the Pariser Platz in Berlin, ca. 1800

"Stand united!"

Bourgeois Society and Family Traditions

David and Liebe Kempler, who owned a café on the Grenadierstrasse in Berlin, with their five children, ca. 1926

In 1789, three years after the death of Moses Mendelssohn, the bourgeoisie asserted itself in the French Revolution. A new social order arose based on freedom and humanity—ideals of the Enlightenment which called many of the previous values into question, such as the inborn privileges of the upper classes. The equality of the Jews was firmly anchored in the new constitution. Throughout all of Europe, a middle class arose as a social stratum and form of living. A secure basis for living, a rational way of life founded in work, achievement, duty, and diligence, the high value placed upon education, culture, and science as well as a basic liberal attitude became the ideal virtues of the bourgeois society. An individually responsible commitment to the community also formed a part of the bourgeois identity. These were all characteristics and values traditionally passed on in Jewish families, as well. Under these fundamental preconditions, many Jewish families, businessmen, and scholars played a considerable role in the development of a bourgeois middle class.

Images of Family

Liberalization and the increasing dominance of economic factors within the hierarchy of living values exerted a strong pressure for change. The family, which had always stood at the center of Jewish life, also had to reorient itself in the face of a changing reality. For the Jewish community, this process was characterized by the development of the middle class nuclear family, which occurred earlier here than in other social strata.

    The more the demands of modern economic life came into conflict with religious practice, the more responsibility domestic life took on in terms of preserving tradition. The family had always been the place where children were instructed in questions of faith and initiated into the rites and customs of Judaism, where Jewish identity was reinforced and conserved. The split between acculturation and the preservation of tradition experienced across the entire Jewish community had to be endured above all within the family.

    An important aspect of family life was the choice of partner. Marriage not only meant a union

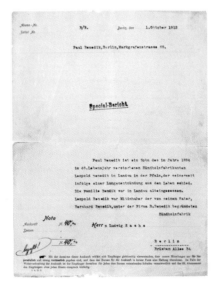
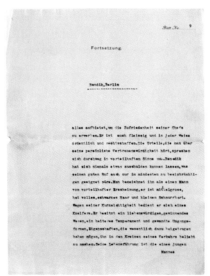
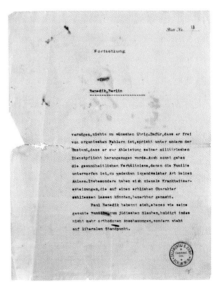

Detective report on a future son-in-law, Paul Benedick,
Berlin, October 1, 1912

Portrait of the Manheimer Family, painting by Julius Moser, ca. 1850

left: Clara Arons, née Goldschmidt, portrait by Philipp Arons, ca. 1860

between two people, but also the consolidation of two families. For this reason, the choice of bride or bridegroom was always a family decision which had to be made carefully. Not infrequently, private detective agencies were employed in order to get a more precise idea of the living conditions of the prospective in-laws regarding their level of education, social standing, and religiousness. The trousseau and the determination of the dowry were a part of the marriage contract, as well, and often provided the groom with a basis for founding a professional existence. The dowry also, however, secured the woman's living should the marriage fail. According to the Talmud, "it is good for both to be married"—when married

life threatened to turn into torture, however, a divorce by mutual consent was permitted. The trousseau became a status symbol in middle class families— with towels and kitchen appliances, books, furniture, and art objects, the young wife was equipped for life.

In order to strengthen the network of relations, candidates for marriage were usually sought within the Jewish community, not seldom among the immediate family circle. The betrothed often first got to know each other through a correspondence carried on during their engagement. In keeping with the romantic ideal of a "marriage for love," the betrothal letters were decorated with hearts, poems, and romantic song texts. The number of mixed marriages, however, also increased considerably in the Wilhelminian Empire; in Berlin of the twenties, every third union involving a Jewish partner was a mixed marriage.

Old family organizations such as the Mendelssohns and the Warburgs in Hamburg, the Bleichröders in Berlin, the Oppenheims in Cologne, or the Rothschilds in Frankfurt counted among the wealthiest families of the Empire, thanks to their well established, successful private banks. Their representative style of living, for instance in the villas of Berlin's Tiergarten quarter or in Grunewald—together with cook, governess and chauffeur, a carefully furnished salon and study, with social events, dinners, and home balls—gave expression to the living culture of the grande bourgeoisie.

Along with the process of secularization, numerous symbols from the non-Jewish environment gained entrance into Jewish families.

Gerson Bleichröder,
portrait by Emile Charles Wauters, 1888

below: Small wooden box filled with linden leaves
that have been cut into heart shapes and inscribed, 1891

Joyful

To be joyful,
miserable,
thoughtful;
To grasp,
to long for
in fearful, suspended agony;
Singing unto heaven,
afflicted unto death—
Happy
is alone the soul
that loves.

JOHANN WOLFGANG VON GOETHE
This poem is inscribed on one of the linden leaves.

Hanukkah, the eight day-long holiday of lights which recalls the victory of the Maccabeans over the Syrians and the renewed consecration of the temple, is celebrated on the 25th day of Kislev, the ninth month of the Jewish calendar, and hence in November or December. A new custom came into being in religiously liberal families whose children wanted to be a part of the Advent and Christmas joy of their class mates: "Weihnukkah," or a mixture between Christmas and Hanukkah. Both holidays were celebrated, with the children opening their gifts on Christmas Eve and the decoration of a tree. Theodor Herzl, the founder of Zionism, wrote on December 24, 1895: "I was just lighting the Christmas tree with my children when Güdemann came by. He seemed annoyed by the 'Christian' custom. Well, I won't be pressured! But for all I care, it can be called the Hanukkah tree—or the winter solstice, for that matter."

The Bourgeois Upbringing

In Jewish life, education was traditionally written in capital letters. While in Prussia only eight percent of all children received an education beyond elementary school, which went up to the age of fourteen, 60 percent of all Jewish children enjoyed further education. On the average, even young Jewish girls received a better education than other daughters of the bourgeoisie. For the sons, a degree in higher education including high school and university study was the indispensable precondition for a career in bourgeois business life. Girls were sent to higher daughters' schools where they were instructed in subjects such as literature, music, French, and handicraft. In the framework of

The Siblings Albert and Julie Rathenau, and Jenny and Gustav Rathenau, two dual portraits by Leopold Bendix, 1845

"Darwinian," a caricature published in the magazine Schlemiel, 1904

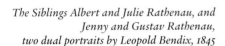

Darwinistisches.

economic prosperity, new professional perspectives opened up. Many now no longer followed in their fathers' footsteps, as had been customary for generations, but chose an academic, artistic, or intellectual profession instead. Among the more prominent examples of the early 20th century are the painter Max Liebermann and the cultural historian Aby Warburg. But many of the Jewish bourgeois sons, such as for example Alfred Kerr and Theodor Wolff, also turned to journalism, and especially to the liberal press of the publishing houses Ullstein and Mosse. They all belonged to the educated elite, yet remained connected to the economic middle class through their families. The lawyer's and doctor's professions were considered to be especially attractive; in 1925, 26 percent of the lawyers and 15 percent of the doctors in the German Empire came from the Jewish community.

It is self-evident that German culture formed a central component of the bourgeois educational canon. As lovers of the classics, admirers of Goethe or enthusiastic fans of Richard Wagner's music, parents initiated their children into cultural life early on through concerts, home music evenings, and poetry recitals. "Mother spent a lot of time with us," the Hamburg banker Max M. Warburg (1867–1946) related of his early family years; she "took care to… oversee our school work and strictly urged us to use our time well. We were never allowed to sit around and chat. She… had a strong sense of duty." In his letters to his sons, the doctor Markus Mosse (1808–1865) strongly emphasized the unwavering cohesion of the family. In a letter to Rudolf, who was at that time just beginning his career as a bookseller in Berlin, he wrote: "Our joys and sorrows in this world are in solidarity among ourselves"; a letter to his sons Theodor and Salomon, who had founded the undergarment business "Gebrüder Mosse" in Berlin, closes with the appeal: "Stand united, united, united!" Solidarity, discipline and ambition, a sense of duty and thrift—the catalogue of virtues which Jewish parents endeavored to pass on to their

The five brothers, Aby, Max, Paul, Felix and Fritz Warburg, ca. 1890

children was that of the bourgeoisie. The insignia of the bourgeois childhood reflect this community of values, from the silver savings box and the lovingly illustrated autograph book to the carefully kept journals and the herbarium.

Public Commitment

In Judaism, charity and social commitment were always considered to be a duty to the community. At the same time, they offered a possibility for heightening the family's social esteem. One of the early charitable organizations was the Gesellschaft der Freunde or Society of Friends, founded in 1792 by Joseph Mendelssohn (1770–1848), one of Moses Mendelssohn's sons. Its job was to support members

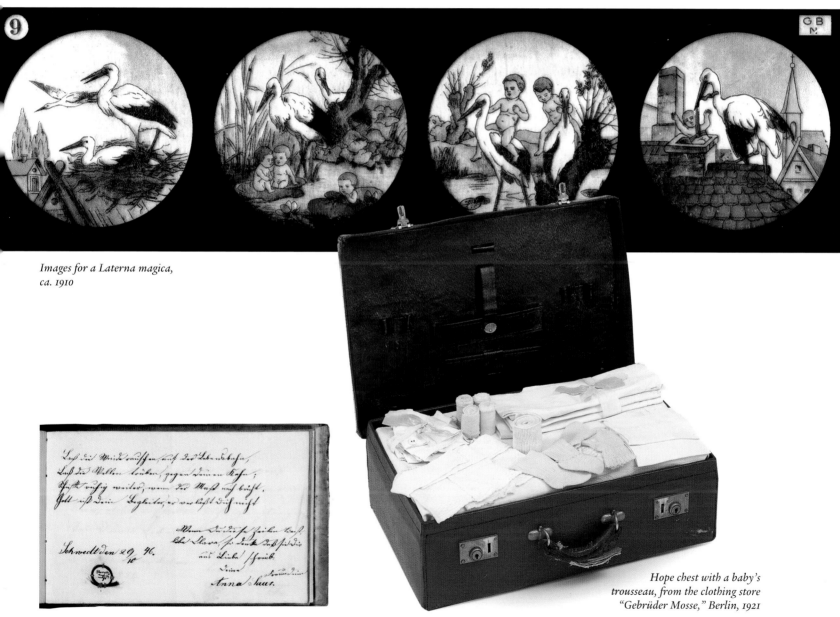

Images for a Laterna magica,
ca. 1910

Autograph book kept by Livia Cohen,
mid-19th century

Hope chest with a baby's
trousseau, from the clothing store
"Gebrüder Mosse," Berlin, 1921

in social and financial states of emergency, but also
to spread and assert the aims of the Enlightenment
in the spirit of Moses Mendelssohn. During the early
years, young sons of the bourgeoisie who were not
yet established met here independently of their
religious persuasion; later, influential persons such
as Emil Rathenau or Gerson von Bleichröder
counted among its 500 members. After the National
Socialists removed the art collection amassed by the
society over the course of years from Berlin's
National Gallery, some of its members relocated
their paintings to the Jewish Museum founded in
1933—the last traces of which were lost after the
museum was closed in 1938. In 1935, the Society of
Friends was banned and its property seized.
Restitution proceedings in the fifties failed.

Influential patrons such as the businessman
James Simon (1851–1932) transformed the cultural
and social landscape. Berlin's museums have Simon
to thank for their Renaissance collections as well as
for important archaeological finds, for example the
excavations of Tell el Amarna, which yielded the bust
of Queen Nefertiti dating from 1350 B.C.E. He also
donated large sums to social and political concerns
and founded non-profit institutions such as the first
two public baths in Berlin in 1887. Together with
Paul Nathan, Simon called the Hilfsverein der deutschen Juden or Association for the Assistance of

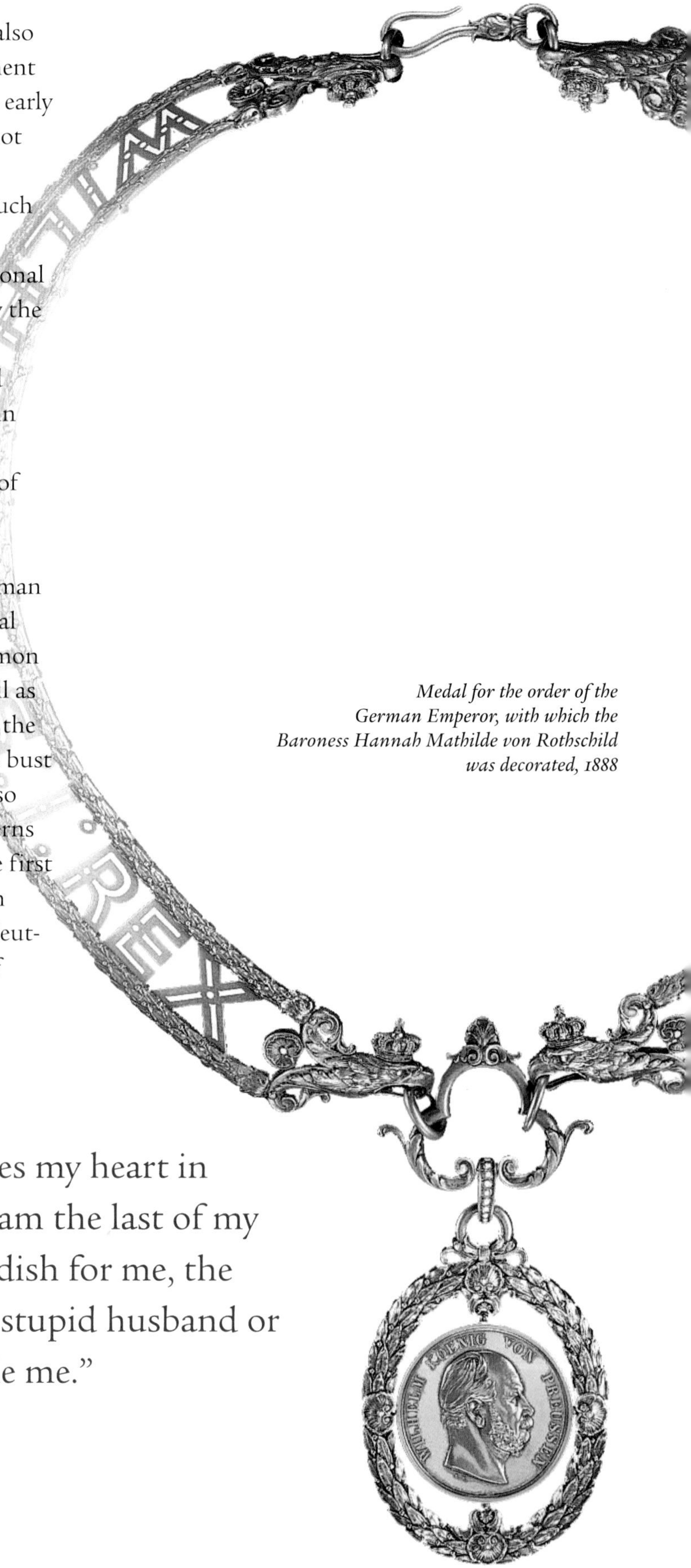

*Medal for the order of the
German Emperor, with which the
Baroness Hannah Mathilde von Rothschild
was decorated, 1888*

"Whenever a melancholic pain tries my heart in
its lonely hours, as I muse that I am the last of my
line and that no one will say kaddish for me, the
thought that I might have had a stupid husband or
an ill-bred child arrives to console me."

BERTHA PAPPENHEIM

German Jews into life in 1901, which enabled more than 200,000 Jews to emigrate out of eastern Europe. Beyond this, he contributed considerably to building up a school system in Palestine and was a co-founder of the technical university in Haifa. The National Socialist regime degraded Simon's collections to "anonymous donations," and many of the works were destroyed in the Second World War.

Since the 19th century, it was also particularly the women of upper middle class families who dedicated themselves to charitable causes, to orphanages, hospitals, and other institutions. Amalie Beer (1776–1854), the mother of the composer Giacomo Meyerbeer, was awarded the Prussian "Luisenorden" for her achievements in caring for the wounded during the German Wars of Liberation of 1816. "Madame Beer" was regarded as being the most hospitable woman of Berlin, as well as the most charitable. "Not a day goes by," said her frequent guest Heinrich Heine, "without her having helped the poor; yes, it seems as though she couldn't go peacefully to bed before completing some noble deed. She donates to the faithful of all religious persuasions, to Jews, Christians, Turks, and even to the unfaithful of the worst sort. She is tireless in charity and appears to regard this as her loftiest call in life."

The foundations of the Rothschild family were renowned. Louise and her sister-in-law, Baroness Hannah Mathilde Rothschild, sponsored children's homes, orphanages, soup kitchens, and sanatoriums. Hannah Mathilde Rothschild (1832–1924), who also founded non-denominational organizations and looked after unwed women regardless of their religious persuasion, received the "Wilhelmsorden" from the emperor for her extraordinary social commitment.

At the turn of the century, charity offered women the possibility to become politically active. The first women's associations striving for an im-

provement in the education of women arose in liberal as well as in orthodox communities. Rahel Goitein (1880–1963), one of the four pupils of the first female high school graduating class in the Kaiserreich, stated in her graduation speech of 1899 that it was the "desire for learning, for knowledge that pointed the way for us"; another consideration was even stronger, however: "we want a profession, we want a place in life." Goitein was the first female student in the medical department in Heidelberg and later opened a medical practice as the first woman to receive a doctorate. Following the death of her husband in 1933, she emigrated to Palestine with the two youngest of her five children.

In 1917, with 200 local associations and around 44,000 members, the Jüdische Frauenbund or Jewish Women's Association, founded in 1904 by Bertha Pappenheim, formed one of the largest Jewish organizations. The Jüdische Frauenbund was a part of the middle class women's movement whose moderate feminism many Jewish women shared. It saw itself, however, as a decidedly Jewish organization which, due to its public influence, was in a position to call attention to necessary reforms while promoting Jewish self-confidence at the same time. In a public appeal for continued support of the emancipation ideal, Henriette Fürth (1897–1930) wrote in 1911: "We are not only women; we are Jewish women. And as long as this epithet continues to imply a distinction of disparagement, we must continue to fight."

Bertha Pappenheim

Bertha Pappenheim (1859–1936) was the most important representative of the Jewish women's movement around the turn of the 20th century. Born into a Jewish orthodox family in Vienna, she dedicated her life to the education of Jewish women and girls and the improvement of their situation in life. Her aims were the emancipation of women and, especially, combating the international trade in young girls. In 1904 she founded the Jüdischer Frauenbund or Jewish Women's Association, and published numerous articles and pamphlets on the political and social situation of Jewish women and girls as well as the position of women in Judaism.

"Dead silence can be a deadly sin"

One of her major causes was the battle against the trade of young girls and the prostitution of Eastern European Jews fleeing westwards from the pogroms in czarist Russia following 1881. Poverty combined with a lack of civil rights and work opportunities forced a large number of these young Jewish women into the organized human trade. From 1903 onwards, Bertha Pappenheim traveled frequently to Galicia to establish aid organizations both there and in Germany. She wrote untiringly, bringing these issues to public attention.

"I imagine … two small houses …"

In 1907 Bertha Pappenheim founded the Home of the Jüdische Frauenbund in Neu-Isenburg near Frankfurt am Main, an educational community centered around four buildings. Originally conceived as a refuge and educational home for single mothers from throughout Germany, Neu-Isenburg soon took in pregnant women, orphans, and young people, and later became a training center for Jewish girls after the National Socialist law of 1933 prevented Jews from training for professions in the public sector.

During the November pogrom in 1938, the Neu-Isenburg Home was set on fire. The members of the staff were deported to Theresienstadt in March 1942; the thirty children that had remained under their care at this time were murdered in Theresienstadt and Auschwitz.

left: Bertha Pappenheim, 1889

below: Flyer offering advice and assistance to girls traveling alone, in German, Yiddish and Polish, circulated by Bertha Pappenheim in the 1920s

Emigrants on a HAPAG-steamship, 1908

"The People of Learning excluded women from Jewish intellectual life, from its sources; women were handed specially prepared morsels to believe in and act upon, without knowing why."

Bertha Pappenheim wanted to reform the role of women in Judaism. She fought for the equal rights, self-determination, and autonomy of Jewish women, but she also consciously compensated the loss of female Jewish tradition. She helped a great number of girls retrieve their cultural and religious roots, allowing them to find a place for themselves in the Jewish community.

The Invisible Past

During her adolescence, Bertha Pappenheim contributed to medical history under the pseudonym "Anna O." in the "Studies on Hysteria" (1895) by Josef Breuer and Sigmund Freud. After many years of caring for her father until his death, she had become psychologically ill. Freud referred to Bertha Pappenheim as "the real founder of the psychoanalytical method."

In later life, she adamantly opposed any form of psychoanalytical treatment for the girls entrusted to her care.

Passing on the tradition: the weekly celebration of Shabbat at the home of the Jewish Women's Association

underlay: Bertha Pappenheim, ca. 1905

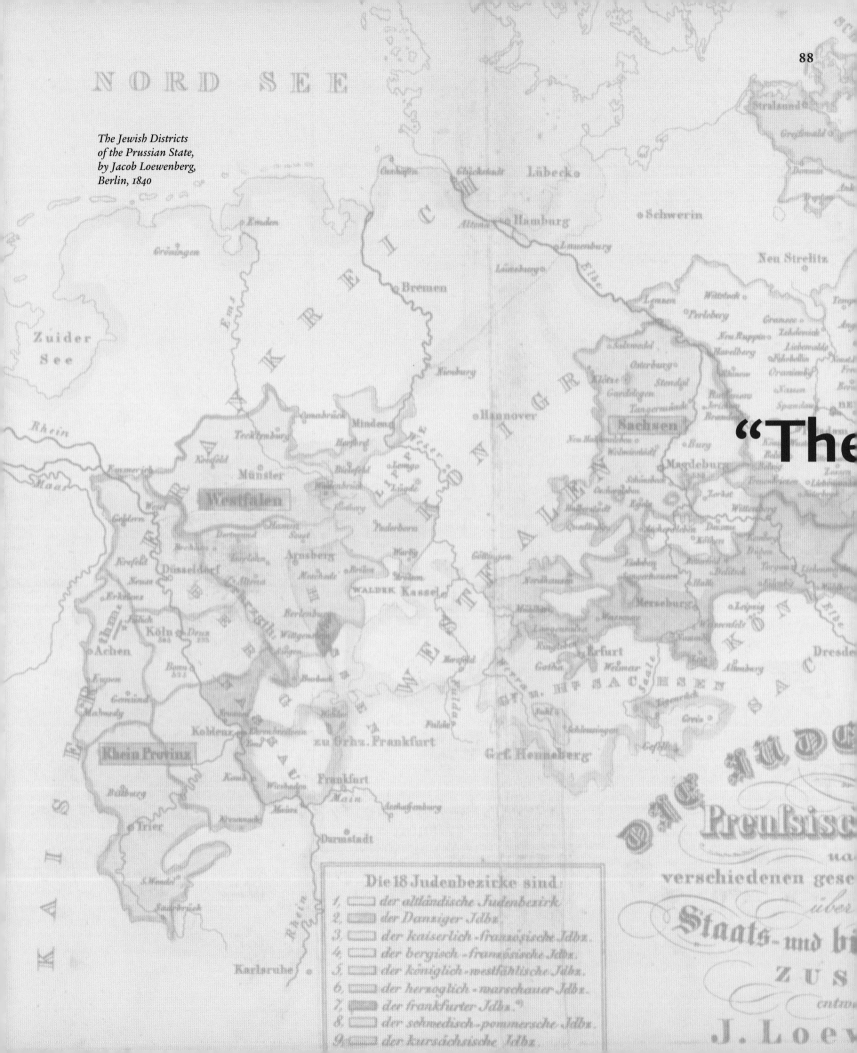

The Jewish Districts
of the Prussian State,
by Jacob Loewenberg,
Berlin, 1840

NORD SEE

Zuider
See

"The

Die 18 Judenbezirke sind:

1. der altländische Judenbezirk
2. der Danziger Jdbz.
3. der kaiserlich-französische Jdbz.
4. der bergisch-französische Jdbz.
5. der königlich-westfälische Jdbz.
6. der herzoglich-warschauer Jdbz.
7. der frankfurter Jdbz.
8. der schwedisch-pommersche Jdbz.
9. der kursächsische Jdbz.

Die Judenbezirke
Preußische

verschiedenen gese

Staats- und bi

Z U S

J. Loev

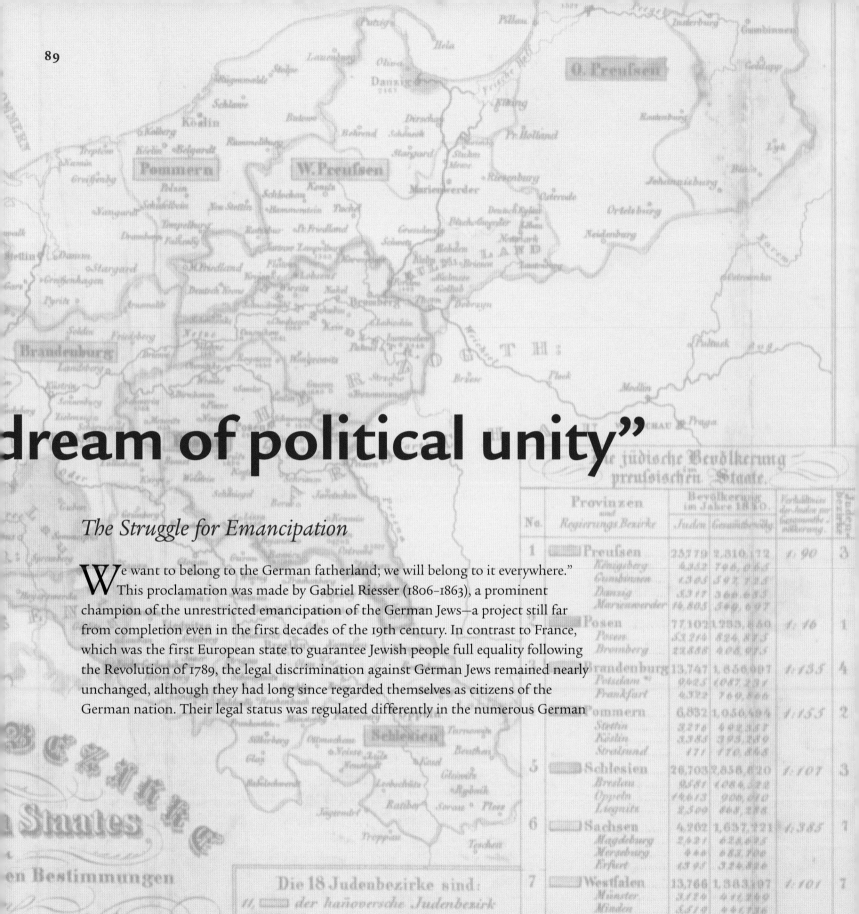

dream of political unity"

The Struggle for Emancipation

We want to belong to the German fatherland; we will belong to it everywhere."
This proclamation was made by Gabriel Riesser (1806–1863), a prominent
champion of the unrestricted emancipation of the German Jews—a project still far
from completion even in the first decades of the 19th century. In contrast to France,
which was the first European state to guarantee Jewish people full equality following
the Revolution of 1789, the legal discrimination against German Jews remained nearly
unchanged, although they had long since regarded themselves as citizens of the
German nation. Their legal status was regulated differently in the numerous German

lands, kingdoms, and principalities; they were still required to pay protection fees and special levies, were excluded from public office and from teaching professions at universities, and were subject to considerable limitations in their rights of residence and in marriage.

Even the committed involvement of influential advocates such as the high Prussian official Christian Wilhelm von Dohm (1751–1820) initially evinced little effect; Dohm regarded progressive equality to be a necessity dictated by the raison d'état, one which would enable "the Jews" to become "more useful members of the bourgeois society" and "more serviceable to our states." In his paper inspired by Friedrich Nicolai and Moses Mendelssohn, "On the Civil Improvement of the Jews," Dohm had

Prussian Emancipation Edict, Berlin, March 11, 1812

already appealed to the decision makers in Prussia and other German territories in 1781 to grant Jewish citizens equality, freedom of religion, and full economic freedom. While Dohm's demands found many supporters, they met with resistance in the Prussian state machinery.

With the victory of the French armies and the occupation of German territories by Napoleon's troops, the political and legal situation changed. After Prussia was forced to surrender large areas to Napoleon, some German lands obtained progressive constitutions which also accorded equality to the Jews; an example of this was the Kingdom of Westphalia (1807–1813) under the rule of Napoleon's brother Jérome, into whose service Dohm had entered.

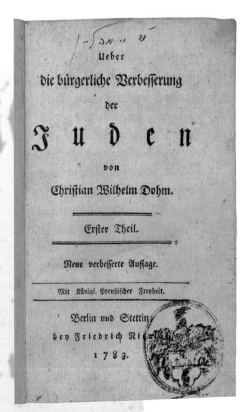

Christian Wilhelm von Dohm, "On the Civil Improvement of the Jews," Nicolai, Berlin and Stettin, expanded edition 1783

One Step Forward, Two Steps Back

Following the military defeat in Prussia, the discussion over reforms concerning the question of the civil equality of Jews resumed. It was, however, to take a few more years until political consequences were drawn from such demands. The liberal state chancellor Baron Karl August von Hardenberg was the first to present King Friedrich Wilhelm III with a progressive draft for a law which went into effect as a royal edict in modified form on March 11, 1812. Thirty years after Dohm's essay appeared, Prussia declared the Jews to be "subjects and Prussian citizens," thus according them the equality they had fought for for so long.

     The Prussian emancipation edict seemed to signify a decisive breakthrough for the rights of Jewish citizens. Yet the application of the new legal situation proved difficult as many states refused to recognize the legitimacy of Hardenberg's "Frenchifying" legal concepts. Only three years later at the Vienna Congress, where the European state system was restructured and the German Confederation established, the project of extending the emancipation edict to all forty member states of the German Confederation failed. The mood changed, and the ideals of the Enlightenment gave way to a reaction growing among parts of the German bourgeoisie. Representatives of German Romanticism such as Clemens von Brentano and Achim von Arnim already turned publicly against the "French Hegemony" in 1812, the year the emancipation edict went into effect—and thus against the emancipation of the Jews. Brentano, for instance, had remarked in a speech before the Christlich-deutsche Tischgesellschaft (the Christian German Dining Association), that the Jews, "those flies left over from the Egyptian plagues," were easily to be lured with "disgust, Enlightenment, and humanitarianism, with rabbit pelts and whitefish."

     Statements made by leading intellectuals and anti-Jewish writings did not fail to hit their mark. In August of 1819, pogroms recalling the medieval per-

Hepp ! Hepp !

above: "Hepp! Hepp!," copper engraving by Michael Voltz, 1819

below: Anti-Jewish flyer from Hamburg, 1819

secutions erupted in several states. The mob plundered Jewish houses in many major cities of the Empire and set fire to synagogues, crying "Hepp! Hepp!" and "Jew, go to Hell!" Even the legislature recoiled far behind the emancipation edict of 1812: from 1819 on, Christian children were no longer allowed to attend Jewish schools, and in 1822, Jews were excluded from the higher ranks of the army. The recent restrictions, however, also provoked resistance, causing the debate of the "Jewish Question" and of political and legal equality to flare up once again.

above: *Bronze Medal of Honor awarded to Gabriel Riesser, 1836*

right: *Honorary lidded cup dedicated in 1847 by the Rhineland Jews to the banker Abraham Oppenheim of Cologne (1804–1878), as a gift for his activism in the First Unified State Assembly in Berlin*

The Revolution of 1848

In the fight for freedom, civil rights, and national unity, numerous Jewish individuals became involved in the civil revolution of 1848. In May of the same year, nine Jewish representatives belonged to the first freely elected parliament, the National Assembly in the Paulskirche in Frankfurt am Main. The politically moderate Hamburg lawyer Gabriel Riesser was its vice president for some time. Of the firm conviction that it was possible to be a Jew and a German at the same time, Riesser placed his wager on the German national state: "If with one hand you were to offer me emancipation, which all my most intimate desires strive towards, and with the other the realization of the wonderful dream of political unity, I would choose the latter without a second thought, because I am firmly and deeply convinced that the one is contained in the other." After he was neither able to become a private instructor at the University of Heidelberg, nor to be called to the bar as a lawyer in Hamburg, he founded a newspaper bearing the provocative title *The Jew*, in which he commented upon the German parliament debates over the rights of Jews. In 1860, only a few years before his death, he was named Obergerichtsrat or high legal counsel, becoming the first Jew in

"The *truth*, as history teaches, has never been prejudicial to the state; only the *obfuscation* of truth. No outspoken writer has ever endangered a government, only his *persecution*."

JOHANN JACOBY

Germany to hold judicial office. It was thanks to Riesser's contribution that the democratic constitution passed in 1849 contained the decisive clause in paragraph 16 of the "Fundamental Rights of the German People": "The enjoyment of civil rights is to be neither influenced nor limited by religious persuasion." Over the course of the following weeks, similar laws on equality were proclaimed in twenty states. Yet the revolution failed, and the progressive constitution never went into effect. The Königsberg doctor Johann Jacoby (1805–1877), who played a central role in the democratic movement in Germany, regarded himself as Riesser's "comrade in belief and misfortune." For Jacoby, the equality of all Jews was a "holy duty" which could only, however, be realized as a part of the general fight for freedom. "Just as I myself am a Jew and a German at one and the same time," Jacoby wrote, "thus can the Jew in me never be free without the German, nor the German without the Jew, and just as I cannot separate myself, so too can I not separate the freedom of the one from the other." His pamphlet of 1841, in which he summarized the program of the democratic opposition in Prussia and demanded the realization of the promise of a constitution, brought him a sentence of three years' detention in a fortress; a few years later, he was arrested once again for his call for a united democratic representation of the German people. Disappointed over the failure of the assembly in the Paulskirche, Jacoby finally joined the social democratic movement.

"A Safe Harbor at Last"

On July 3, 1869, the Reichstag of the North German Confederation decreed that "all existing limitations on civil rights derived from a difference in religious persuasion are hereby eliminated." After the failure of the revolution of 1848, this law once again represented a breakthrough. When two years later Bismarck "unified" the German lands under the leadership of Prussia, his authority was extended to the whole of the new German Reich. "At last," the Jewish politician Raphael Kosch wrote, "the Jews have entered a safe harbor." After a long period of back and forth, formal equality was finally attained. The years 1848 and 1869–1871 heralded a new era for the Jews: more numerous and more prominent in politics than ever before, they now took their seats as elected officials in the parliaments. Moritz Elstätter, the long-time financial minister of Baden, was the first observant Jew to become a member of government.

Declaration of gratitude by the Rhineland Jews to Abraham Oppenheim, 1847

Minyan or Memorial prayer of a Jewish soldier after the battle of Wörth, engraving by Moritz Daniel Oppenheim, 1872. A Jewish soldier is praying with his comrades on the anniversary of his father's death.

The two most influential German Jewish politicians of the liberal age were Eduard Lasker (1829–1884), a Prussian by conviction, and Ludwig Bamberger (1823–1899), who was born in Mainz. In 1848, both had belonged to the radical wing of the democratic movement. Bamberger was even sentenced to death in his absence and had to flee because of his participation in the Palatine rebellion; in 1868, he returned after nearly twenty years in exile as a successful banker. As members of the National Liberal Party, they had both supported Bismarck's goal of uniting the Empire. In 1866, Lasker formulated the party program and exerted considerable influence on the drafting of a new code of civil law. Bamberger, one of the first directors of the Deutsche Bank, earned credit for creating a unified financial system. In 1878, they each voted for Bismarck's imperial law "against the dangerous aims of social democracy."

Lasker later regretted this step, because the so-called socialists' law signified the end of liberalism. Bismarck had given up the politics of free trade. Lasker and Bamberger, a committed supporter of free trade, to which he ascribed "progress, peace, and freedom," were not reelected. Bismarck's about-face signalized the end of the short-lived emancipatory phase. It helped the conservative forces—who, as the *Allgemeine Zeitung des Judentums* (the General Newspaper of Judaism) wrote, were aiming to "thoroughly bring the principles of the Middle Ages to bear once again"—to attain social influence.

Modern Anti-Semitism

Advocates of anti-modern tendencies within Romanticism had already been fighting against the secularized society, a money-based economy, and the liberal state. Due to their divergent professional structure, the Jewish population was identified with these modern achievements, all the more strongly, in fact, the more a dire economic state and social upheaval nourished disappointment over the promises liberalism had failed to keep since the seventies of the 19th century. The advent of "anti-Semitism" popularized this position among wide circles of society. In contrast to Christian anti-Judaism, Jews were now no longer held in contempt as a religious community, but rather as a "race."

Anti-Semitism became a political movement with the court preacher Adolf Stoecker, whom Emperor Wilhelm I summoned to Berlin in 1874. Stoecker was a clever orator who attracted the masses and, endowed with the virtually official authority of throne and altar, he exerted considerable influence on the conservative society. He founded the Christian Social Workers' Party (later called the Christian Social Party), which found wide support among the middle class and rural population. With the exception of the social democrats, who under August Bebel decidedly distanced themselves from anti-Semitism at their party congress in 1891, anti-Jewish resentment could soon be found in nearly all social milieux at the close of the century: in political Catholicism as well as in the Protestant bourgeoisie, among students and farmers alike, in art and culture as well as in the clerks' union.

After the historian Heinrich von Treitschke, the most influential representative of the science of national German history, coined the phrase "The Jews are our misfortune" in the Prussian Almanac, anti-Semitism became acceptable in academia. Treitschke helped sanction anti-Semitism as a tenet; "whatever he said became respectable," his staunch opponent, the classical historian Theodor Mommsen, said of him. In 1871, Mommsen authored a brief in defense of Judaism together with Rudolf Virchow, Rudolf von Gneist, Johann Droysen, and seventy-six other scientists. Resistance also came from the Jewish side. In 1893, Raphael Löwenfeld (1854–1910) founded the Central-Verein deutscher Staatsbürger jüdischen Glaubens (Central Association of German

Citizens of Jewish Faith) in Berlin, which had the resistance of anti-Semitism as its goal. The purpose of the organization consisted in "gathering together German citizens of Jewish faith, regardless of differences in religious and political direction, and strengthening them in the energetic retention of their civil and social equality as well as in the unwavering preservation of German convictions."

Albertine Mendelssohn-Bartholdy, née Heine, as a Bride, painting by August Theodor Kaselowsky, 1835

Tradition and Change—The Life

As in other religions, there is a religious life cycle in Judaism, as well. Important stations of life such as birth, coming of age, founding a family, and death are marked by a special ceremony integrating the private event into the community.

Brit Milah

A Jew is anyone born to a Jewish mother or who has converted to Judaism according to the Halakhic precepts. The *Brit Milah* or circumcision is regarded as the sign of the covenant with God through which the male child is accepted into the community of Israel. It is normally carried out on the eighth day after birth, because, according to the Torah, Abraham circumcised his son Isaac on the eighth day. The newborn receives his name on the day of the Brit Milah; a girl's name is announced in the synagogue at the first Shabbat service following birth.

Bar and Bat Mitzvah

"A five year-old is mature enough for the Bible, a ten year-old for the *Mishnah*, a thirteen year-old for the fulfillment of the commandments..." (Sayings of the Fathers 5, 24). At the completion of the thirteenth year, the Jewish boy comes of age, becoming a *Bar Mitzvah* or son of the commandments. He is now a full member of the community with all the rights and responsibilities laid down by religious law and is counted in the minyan, the congregation of ten men required to be present for the practice of a religious service.

Girls become religiously mature at the completion of their twelfth year. It used to be expected of girls that they be familiar with running a household in accordance with the kashrut and other Halakhic prescripts concerning the home and the family. Beginning in the 19th century, a ceremony for girls has been introduced in reformed communities—the *Bat Mitzvah*, daughter of the commandments.

Paper cut-out with a representation of the life cycle, presumably Berlin, 1909

Von Stufe zu Stufe.

Wedding canopy by Saskia Weishut-Snapper, made from antique and contemporary fabrics, hand-painted and embroidered, Amsterdam, 2001

Cycle

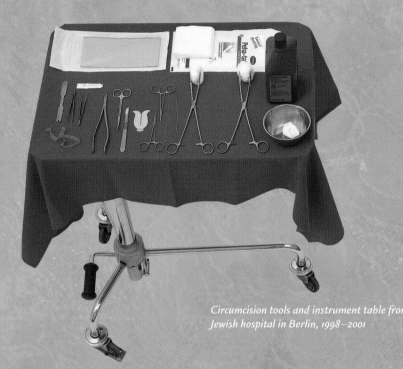

Circumcision tools and instrument table from the Jewish hospital in Berlin, 1998–2001

At the wedding ceremony, the couple stands under the huppah, a wedding canopy which symbolizes the couple's home. As a symbol for married life, "huppah" has come to mean marriage in Hebrew. In the first part of the ceremony (betrothal), the rabbi gives his blessing over the goblet of wine from which the couple drinks. The actual legal ceremony follows there-after: the bridegroom presents the bride with a ring, and the rabbi reads the *ketubbah* or marriage contract. The second part of the ceremony constitutes the marriage. Seven benedictions are pronounced, the couple drinks from the wine once again, and then the bride-groom steps on or smashes a glass in order to recall the destruction of the temple even in the moment of the greatest personal happiness.

Death and Burial

Since the Middle Ages, almost every community has a *hevra kaddisha* (holy society). These burial brother and sisterhoods are there to visit the ill, stand by the dying and arrange a worthy burial after death. Jewish burials are markedly simple; the coffin consists of plain boards, for all humans are alike in death, whether they were rich or poor in life. The traditional concept of the resurrection of the dead calls for a ground burial. For the same reason, Jewish cemeteries are intended for eternity and bear names such as "House of Life" or "House of Eternity." The burial should be carried out on the day of death or at the latest the following day.

Marriage

Marriage and family assume a high position in Judaism, a fact expressed in the wish pronounced for an infant: "May he grow up into the Torah, the *huppah*, and good deeds." Marriage and children are a part of the natural order of life ordained by God. On the wedding day itself, the couple fasts before the ceremony to prepare themselves in dignity for marriage. The wedding ceremony is normally carried out by a rabbi. It can be performed anywhere, in the synagogue or out-doors. The presence of two male witnesses is required.

Rabbi Anton Nehemia Nobel in front of the
synagogue on the Börneplatz in Frankfurt am Main,
ca. 1915

"... to great creations"

The Development of Modern Judaism

Over the course of the European Enlightenment movement, the Jews began viewing their own traditions with a new eye. At the same time, the desire to integrate themselves into German society grew—and to many, long-standing customs and ways of thinking appeared to be obstructions to this process. Reforms became necessary, also to curb the increasing number of conversions to Christianity that were attractive to many in order to gain access to social, public, or academic positions closed to Jews. Throughout the 19th century, rabbis, theologians, scientists, and philosophers tried out new forms of Judaism corresponding to the changing needs and living conditions of the Jewish population and the expectations of their Christian environment. They combined Jewish traditions with elements of the culture surrounding them, filling them with new life. The modern German Judaism which now arose ultimately became the model for Jewish communities in other parts of the world.

Leopold Zunz, portrait by an unknown artist,
ca. 1875

The Science of Judaism

Under the impression of the "Hepp Hepp" riots, a group of young men came together at the end of 1819 to form the Verein für Kultur und Wissenschaft der Juden (Society for the Culture and Science of the Jews). Among its founding members was the lawyer and Hegel pupil Eduard Gans (1798–1839), who later, in 1825, had been baptized in order to take on a professorship at the Berlin University, and the rabbi and philologist Leopold Zunz (1794–1886), who became the most important representative of the science of Judaism. The poet Heinrich Heine also joined the society. These young intellectuals turned their ttention to the study of Jewish history and its place

To an Apostate

O the pious valor of youth!
How quickly thou art tam'd!
So thou hast, in cool blood,
Been reconcil'd with our dear lords.

Thou'st eaten thy words, and cower
Before the very cross that thou once scorn'd
The very cross that, so few weeks past, thou
Hop'd to trounce and bury in dust!

O this is the deed that all thy reading—
All thy Burke, Haller, Schlegel—
Leads thee to: yesterday's hero
Today washes up a knavish turncoat.

HEINRICH HEINE (1797–1856)
Heine wrote this poem after learning that his friend
Eduard Gans had converted to Christianity. Heine had
himself converted a short while before. The poem was
found among Heine's papers after his death; it is unlikely
that Gans knew of it.

in world history—a high goal connected to the hope of finding a form of Judaism which they could identify with again and which deserved its place in European society.

The Verein disbanded in 1824; it had neither found sufficient support within the Jewish community, nor had it been able to assert itself against growing pressures from outside. Zunz continued to develop the concept of the science of Judaism. He authored its first significant work, a paper concerned with one of the central themes of the reform debate and published in 1832, entitled "The Performance of the Religious Service of the Jews, Developed Historically." It refuted the standpoint of both the orthodox rabbis and the Prussian government, which held that the German language was not permissible in the Jewish religious service. An important project of the science of Judaism was the compilation of a Jewish encyclopedia. In 1841, Zunz wrote to the publisher Bernhard Beer that a work of this kind "on Jewish matters" required time: "…thus, the powers should first concentrate themselves in order to produce great creations."

Reform of the Religious Service

Since the beginning of the 19th century, efforts at reform had been focused on the religious service. The reformers sought to introduce more order, more dignity and ceremoniousness into the synagogue, and oriented themselves along the Protestant model. One of the first attempts to call a reformed devotional into life was undertaken by the Royal Westphalian Consistory of Israelites in Kassel, where the Jews had been accorded civil rights under the short-lived government of Napoleon's brother Jérome. The Consistory had made it its task to promote an inner reform of Judaism and, consequently, the social integration of Jewish citizens as well.

Silver Torah finials, Berlin, ca. 1763

Israel Jacobsohn, portrait by Georg Friedrich Adolph Schöner, ca. 1820

Israel Jacobson (1768–1828), a wealthy banker and champion of emancipation who had founded a liberal Jewish school in the small village of Seesen in the Harz mountains, became its president. In 1810, Jacobson annexed a synagogue to his school, the so-called Jacob's Temple. Hebrew and Latin Bible verses in the portal pediment indicated that Christianity and Judaism had much in common. On the roof, a small bell tower chimed at the hour. For the first time, a Jewish religious service was accompanied by choral singing, German hymns, and organ music. Many prayers which had been traditionally spoken by the entire community were exclusively reserved for the *cantor*. Jacobson introduced a sermon in the German language, meant less to serve the purposes of exhortation than edification, as well as a confirmation ceremony for boys and girls. Heated discussions broke out, above all over the introduction of organ music, rejected by the orthodoxy as a Christianization of the religious service. Jacobson led the consecration service in his temple himself. In the closing prayer, he gave expression to his hope of a coming together of Christianity and Judaism: "above all else, however, let us realize whole-heartedly that we are the brothers of the faithful of all other divine doctrines… brothers at last, which under Your direction are transforming towards a common goal and shall finally… meet on the same path."

When the kingdom of Westphalia and with it the Consistory of Israelites was dissolved in 1813, Jacobson went to Berlin. There, on the occasion of his son's Bar Mitzvah, he established a religious service following the Seesen model in his home. Attendance soon became so high that the synagogue had to be moved to the more spacious home of the sugar manufacturer Jakob Herz Beer (1769–1825), the father of the composer Giacomo Meyerbeer. In December 1823, the Beer Temple, in which Leopold Zunz also held services, was closed on the orders of the Prussian king. Complaints on the part of orthodox community members had been submitted to the government, which responded with a "highest cabinet order" prohibiting any changes in the form and language of the Jewish religious service. Thus, for the time being, the attempts at reform in Prussia were put to an end.

Religious Positions

In the 1830s, academically educated rabbis began working on designs for the renewal of the Jewish religion. Divergent positions between reform and orthodoxy came into being, whose representatives and followers carried on heated discussions among one another.

The most important representative of the Jewish reform movement, Abraham Geiger (1810–

Torah shield, partially gilded silver, by Casimir Ernst Burcky, Berlin, ca. 1796

1874), saw Judaism as a living religion in a constant process of change and further development. Wherever it appeared necessary, old forms should be replaced by new ones. For reasons concerning the politics of emancipation, Geiger clearly turned against the nationalist elements of the Jewish hope in the messiah: "Judaism… must be separated… from all elements of national aspiration; … rather, we declare in a most heart-felt way that we belong to the land we live in as our fatherland."

For the Jewish community of Breslau, Geiger published a prayer book in 1854 that became the basis for the majority of liberal prayer books in use in Germany. He had either rewritten or crossed out all parts referring to a return to Zion, the hope in a personified messiah and the sacrificial ceremony in the temple in Jerusalem. Geiger had only been able to assume his office as rabbi in Breslau in 1840 against the bitter resistance of the orthodox head rabbi Salomon Titkin, who had even turned to the chief commissioner of the Breslau police to have Geiger's election declared invalid. The fight between the liberal and the orthodox factions in the community was ultimately resolved by the establishment of two separate cultural commissions which each had free hand in the choice of their rabbis, in the form of their service and religious instruction.

Samson Raphael Hirsch (1808–1888), Geiger's opponent and college friend from Bonn, founded a modern orthodoxy. This neo-orthodoxy was concerned with harmonizing the goals of emancipation and the acquisition of a basic education with traditional Judaism. Hirsch saw no contradiction between Jewish tradition and modern culture; on the contrary: it was precisely the fulfillment of the commandments and the exemplary life according to divine doctrine which were Israel's mission in the world. Hirsch's slogan was "Torah in Derech Erez," the connection between a life faithful to the Torah with the active participation in German culture, economy and society.

Abraham Geiger,
posthumous portrait by Lesser Ury,
ca. 1907

"I love Germany, despite that its public institutions make me an outcast because I am a Jew.
Does Love require reason? I feel entwined with its science, with all its intellectual and moral gravity; and who can sever the nerve of his own existence with impunity?"

ABRAHAM GEIGER

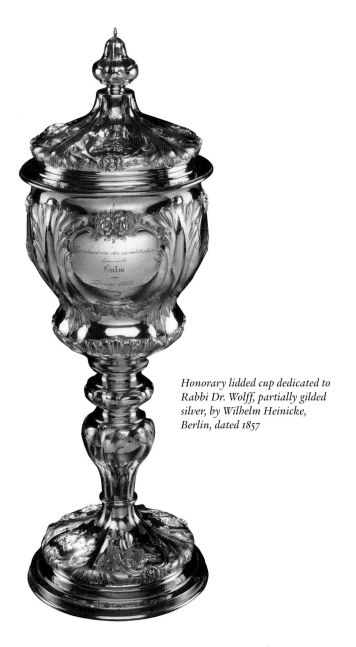

*Honorary lidded cup dedicated to
Rabbi Dr. Wolff, partially gilded
silver, by Wilhelm Heinicke,
Berlin, dated 1857*

In August 1851, Hirsch, a charismatic orator, took office as the rabbi of the Israelitische Religionsgesellschaft (Israelite Religion Society) in Frankfurt am Main. Its members had come together because they felt pushed to the fringes of the main community dominated by the members of the reform movement. The Religionsgesellschaft founded its own schools in which worldly as well as religious subjects were taught. Hirsch introduced a German sermon and choral singing into the religious service, and the rabbi's robe he wore hardly differed from that of his liberal colleagues. Opponents of these novelties defamed Hirsch's position as "Schinken-orthodoxie" or ham orthodoxy. Yet it was precisely these changes in ceremony which once again made traditional Judaism accessible to many. Respected and wealthy citizens of the city such as the banking family Rothschild counted among the members of the Israelitische Religionsgesellschaft.

With the support of the liberal Jewish representative Eduard Lasker, Hirsch put the so-called secession law through the Prussian parliament in 1876, a law which enabled Jews to secede from their local communities and to join a separate community without losing their affiliation with Judaism. Yet to Hirsch's bitter disappointment, the majority of the members of his community did not take this step—they preferred to remain in the main community along with their membership in the Israelitische Religionsgesellschaft.

Zacharias Frankel (1801–1875), who had grown up in Prague and had studied in Pest in Hungary, became an early thinker of the conservative or "positive-historical" direction in German Judaism. He rejected radical reform as well as closed-minded traditionalism, thus becoming the "man of the middle right." He promoted moderate renewals insofar as they could be legitimized from within Judaism itself. In his programmatic essay of 1844, "On Reforms in Judaism," he wrote: "Reconciliation of faith with life, progress within faith, preservation and cultivation, the regeneration of Judaism out of and through itself—this is the circle within which our efforts should move: whatever lies outside of this has ceased to be Judaism; and whoever considers this circle too broad prefers stagnation and dissolution to life and activity."

In 1836, Frankel was named head rabbi in Dresden, and in 1854 he took over the leadership of the newly founded Jewish Theological Seminary in Breslau, the first modern educational establishment for rabbis. The historically critical study of post-Biblical scriptures in the Breslau seminary was new and not customary in the traditional Talmud schools. Along with their seven-year schooling, the rabbi candidates were also required to complete university study. Graduates of the Breslau seminary found positions as rabbis and teachers in numerous Jewish communities in Germany, thus assuring the spread of Frankel's ideas. The Jewish Theological Seminary became the model for similar institutions around the world, among them the influential Jewish Theological Seminary in New York.

"Not since the days of Paul of Tarsus, has Judaism experienced an inner enemy who has so shaken its entire structure to the foundation"—thus was the judgment the historian Heinrich Graetz passed on one of the most radical and controversial representatives of reformed Judaism: Samuel Holdheim (1806–1860). Holdheim had grown up in the orthodox milieu of the province of Posen and did not come into contact with the reform movement until the age of thirty. Under Holdheim's

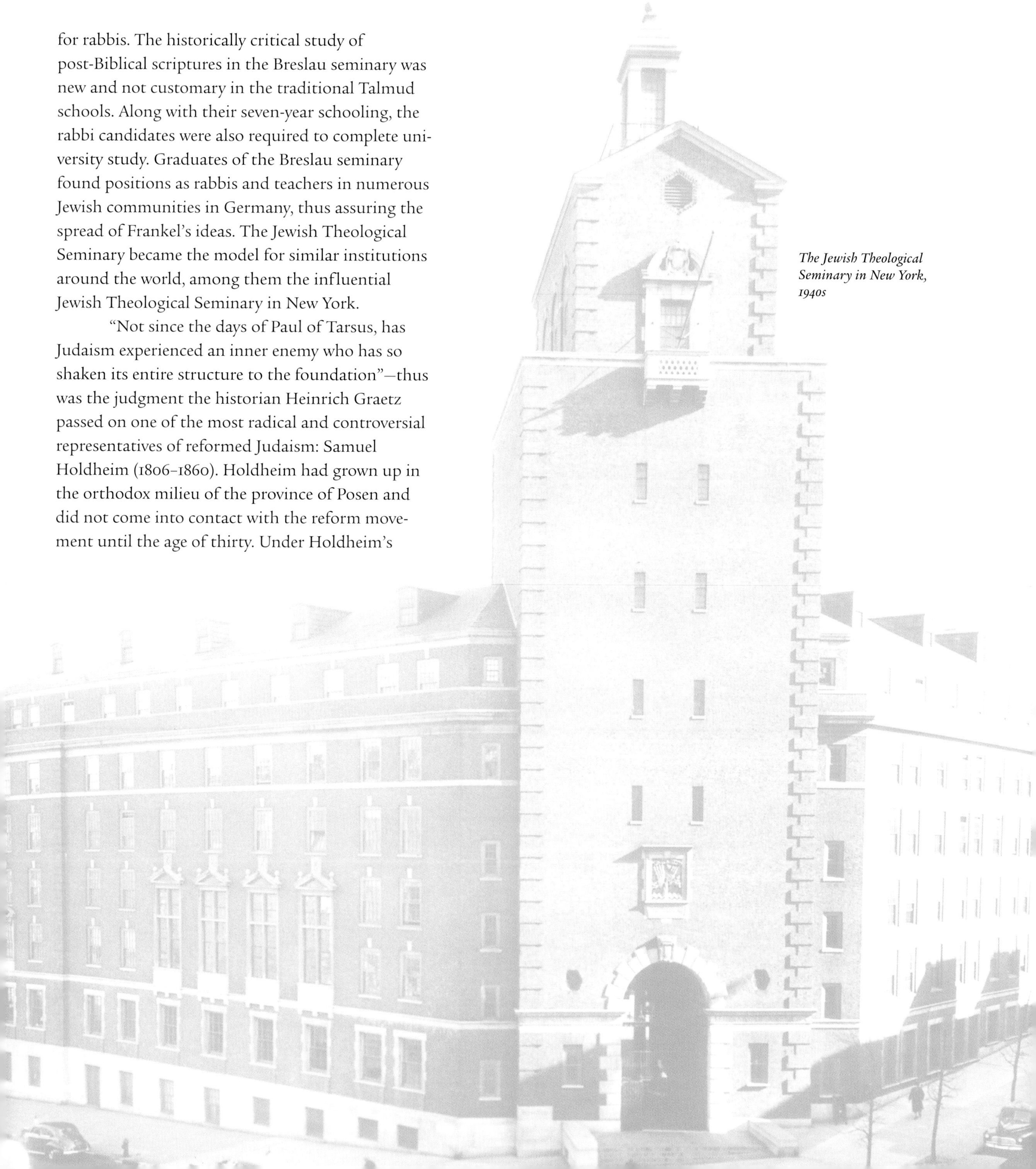

The Jewish Theological Seminary in New York, 1940s

leadership, the reformed Jewish community of Berlin introduced spectacular innovations into their religious services in 1847: most of the men prayed without head coverings; the women were not seated in the galleries, but rather with the men in the actual synagogue room, separated only by the center aisle; the prayers were almost entirely recited in German; and the main religious service was shifted from the Shabbat to Sunday. Organ music and a mixed choir accompanied the service.

For Holdheim, religious law had lost all of its binding character. Judaism should adapt entirely to the religious needs of modern Jews: "Because we are true and sincere to our father religion, but do not love it in a passionate blindness, so are we all the more sincere and deeply inspired by the wish ... to see every foreign element which does not belong to its essential, spiritually moral content depart from

*Model for the synagogue
in the Glockengasse in Cologne,
Ernst Friedrich Zwirner,
architect*

its unnatural connection to it." Yet Holdheim's rigorism found only very few supporters, even within the reformed circles. After his death, his opponents tried to prevent his burial in the part of the cemetery reserved for rabbis, albeit unsuccessfully. Abraham Geiger held the funeral address.

Jewish Schools

The Freyschule, founded for Jewish boys in Berlin by the rationalists David Friedländer and Isaac Daniel Itzig in 1778, was considered to be a model for modern Jewish education. Only a few years after the decree of 1819, however, when Christian pupils were prohibited from attending Jewish schools, they lost public support for the school and had to abandon it. Other schools had arisen according to its model, such as the Royal Wilhelmsschule in Breslau or the Herzogliche Franzschule in Dessau, which also admitted girls and taught according to the pedagogic ideas of the Christian philanthropists. The Philanthropin, founded in 1804 with the help of Mayer Amschel Rothschild in Frankfurt am Main, developed into the most famous Jewish school, breaking with traditional education in a more radical way than the other schools. In the middle of the 19th century, it became a nondenominational school in the model of the Freyschule once again, where Jewish teachers and pupils were the equals of their Christian counterparts.

While the public took a lively interest in the foundings of schools bearing a liberal stamp and these were integrated into the emancipation debate as positive examples for the education of Jews to "useful citizens of the state," modern school attempts on the part of the orthodoxy remained in the background. They, too, opened themselves up to new pedagogic concepts as did the Hachscharath Zwi, founded in 1795 in Halberstadt, or the Talmud-Torah School in Hamburg, which was founded in 1805.

In the second half of the 19th century, however, the share of Jewish pupils at state elementary schools rose considerably, and the gymnasiums and lycées became popular. Apart from a few exceptions, Jewish education declined due to the acculturation and assimilation process of the German Jews.

The various concepts of Jewish education and religious reform had one thing in common: their protagonists shared the conviction that a participation in the political and social life of Germany was possible while retaining their religious and cultural identity at the same time. In the majority of the Jewish communities in Germany, the proponents of reform finally prevailed. The religious contradictions which had determined the inner-Jewish discourse in the 19th century gradually lost meaning. In the Weimar era, they were replaced by the no less heatedly carried on controversies between liberals and Zionists.

"If you ask me ... to confess what drove me, a woman, to become a rabbi: a belief in my calling and my love for mankind ... Everyone of us, man or woman, has a duty to work and create what he can with the gifts God gave him."

REGINA JONAS (1902–1944)
In 1935, Jonas became the first woman to be ordained as a rabbi.

far left: View down the Judengasse in Frankfurt, ca. 1860

left: Dedication of the main synagogue on the Judengasse in Frankfurt, March 23, 1860

underlay: The eastern end of the Judengasse, ca. 1890

"One of the ominous things that troubled the young boy, and certainly the youth as well, was the condition of the Jewish quarter, that was in fact called Judengasse because it consists of little more than a single street that in earlier times ran between the city wall and the moat, wedged in like some kind of bear-pit."

Wavering between fascination and aversion, Johann Wolfgang von Goethe recalls his visits to the overcrowded Judengasse in his hometown, the milling throngs of people, and the unfamiliar language. He started learning *Yiddish*, frequently visited the synagogue, and attended a circumcision, a wedding, and a celebration of *Sukkot*, the feast of the tabernacles.

The Judengasse in Frankfurt

How did this *ghetto* develop? For ages, Frankfurt was the only city that tolerated Jews on a long-term basis. In 1462, Emperor Friedrich III decreed that the Jews should leave their quarters and move outside the city walls, where they settled in dwellings along the strip called "Am Wollgraben." The city of commerce and trade fairs attracted more Jewish families, new buildings were constructed, and by the beginning of the 17th century, there were almost 3000 members in the community. But living conditions deteriorated because the laws banned Jews from buying additional land and compelled them to keep all three gates locked throughout the night. The street became narrower: the people had to build in four rows on either side of the road and increase the number of floors. The front and rear buildings became so intricately interlocked that the windows above certain doors sometimes belonged to different houses. Several families often lived together under one roof because of the lack of space. The road was about 400 meters long and only 3 meters wide at its narrowest points. This let in very little daylight, and the lack of sanitation created additional health hazards including the rapid spread of infectious diseases. As the poet Ludwig Börne, who grew up here, noted ruefully: "Children had no yards, no little gardens behind the houses where they could play their innocent games."

This ghetto with its narrow confines was unique in Germany. It was a realm of infinite contrasts: poor and rich lived side by side, while family festivities and religious festivals, weddings, and circumcision celebrations generated a mutual sense of community and security. In 1761, house numbers were introduced, but the old house signs hanging above the street remained with names such as "The Yellow Rose," "The Golden Crown," and "The Green Shield."

The decline of the ghetto began in 1796, when French troops bombarded the city and half of the houses burned down. Then, in 1808, the gates finally fell. Although the Jewish population still did not have the same rights as Christian citizens, the discriminatory rules that had restricted the lives of the Jewish population for centuries disappeared. In his sermon commemorating the opening of the new synagogue in 1860, Rabbi Leopold Stein called for the demolition of this "atrocious street." By 1884, all the buildings in the Judengasse had disappeared, except for the old home of the Rothschild banking family. This building remained intact until it was destroyed by bombs in 1944.

The Five Rothschild Brothers,
lithograph after paintings
by Moritz Daniel Oppenheimer,
1852

am Main

"Berlin at night": The Leiser shoe store on the Friedrich-strasse, postcard from the 1920s

Berlin bei Nacht.

"Here let me live!"

On the Path to Modernism

The train pulled into Anhalter Station. We had reached Berlin, and I called out: Eli, lord of the angels! Here let me live! Save my soul—I trust in you!" Full of hope, the twenty year-old Alfred Kerr arrived in Berlin in 1887, giving expression to a dynamics which had seized hold of the non-Jewish and even more so the Jewish population in the second half of the 19th century. The aspiring cities, with Berlin at their forefront, became the symbol of a new era dawning, an era of radical change in all traditional living conditions.

The last steps to emancipation—the attainment of legal equality in the new German Empire and the internal reform of Judaism—had been completed during a phase in which the political landscape of central Europe was decisively changing. The tendency towards national unification now prevailing everywhere was favored not least by a dynamics of economic and social growth, which brought the empire an unprecedented upswing: between 1871 and 1910, the population grew from 41 to 65 million; the number of people living in cities doubled, as did the average per capita income; progress in science and technology revolutionized the everyday life of society; new manufacturing procedures founded mass consumerism; new media and services met with an increasingly interested and solvent public; electric light enabled cities to shine more brightly than ever before known, transforming them into magnets for people from the rural surrounding areas, but from further afield as well.

The city of Berlin was at the forefront of this modernization process right from the beginning of industrialization. Through the rapid expansion of the railroad network, Berlin became a central junction; as a result, it developed into Germany's largest industrial city. In 1849, the population numbered 400,000 inhabitants; this figure increased rapidly until it crossed the 2 million mark in 1905. In 1920, when the surrounding towns and outlying districts were joined to found Greater Berlin, it stood at 4 million. The number of Jewish inhabitants in Berlin rose as well, from around 36,000 in 1871 to 144,000 in 1910. That meant that nearly a quarter of all the Jews of Germany resided in the imperial city. They made up a consistent percentage of around four percent of Berlin's population, and around one percent in the entire empire; yet while the community in Berlin grew, other important centers of Jewish life in Germany were shrinking, such as Posen, for example, which up until the 19th century had been the largest Jewish community in Prussia.

The process whereby large sections of German Jewry became bourgeois was simultaneously a process of urbanization that had begun earlier and ran deeper than among the non-Jewish population. The boom of the large cities, with Berlin in the lead as the center for trade, provided a variety of economic possibilities for the Jewish population. While in 1907 a mere 12 percent of the total population

Placard by Louis Oppenheim for the clothing store "S. Adam" in Berlin, 1910-11. Fritz Adam began, in the 1920s, to design sets and costumes for adventure films. After the April Boycott in 1933, he and his family emigrated to London. His son Ken, born in Berlin in 1921 with the name Klaus Adam, continued his father's tradition: films such as "Dr. Strangelove" and the early James Bond movies became legendary with Ken Adam's décor.

underlay: Illustration by Barthold Asendorpf for Georg Hermann's novel "Jettchen Gebert" (1906), ca. 1932, captioned "Return through the Brandenburg Gate." The Geberts spent the summer in Charlottenburg

"Once you go in for ad films, you're lost to the world."

JULIUS PINSCHEWER (1883–1961)
Pioneer of advertising film

> "Now, now, what could happen? It
> can't be all that bad. No one's
> going to die. Berlin is huge. Where
> thousands live, one more can live."

ALFRED DÖBLIN (1878–1957)
Berlin Alexanderplatz

*Salvarsan capsules—
the first medicine for
treating syphilis,
developed by Paul Ehrlich*

worked in trade or transport, statistics on the Jewish working structure point to a 60 percent activity in these fields.

The late 19th and early 20th century saw the continuing social rise of a considerable portion of the Jewish population. Apart from the small wealthy upper class and a somewhat larger lower class, Jews in towns or in the country belonged to the more or less secure middle classes. The push for modernization in Berlin, heralded euphorically in the city itself as "the rise to a metropolis," was carried out with the significant participation of Jewish inhabitants from all social strata. Their above average level of education supported their involvement in the radical renewal of urban structures. In 1911, there were five times as many Jewish students attending the Prussian universities in proportion to the population share Jewish inhabitants comprised in Prussia; 14 percent of Prussia's female students were Jewish.

In stark contrast to the trends of social ascent and academic orientation of Jews especially in Berlin stood the rigid, conservative system attributed to Wilhelm II, which did not generally accept Jews as equals. As far as social contact went, individual exceptions were made, but access to the traditional elite groups of the army, the courts, and administration was for the most part blocked. Thus, above all the younger Jewish generation, who already viewed equality as a natural precondition, was almost inevitably drawn along the path to modernization and reform, to the construing and introduction of new forms of commercial behavior and communication, to new professional fields, branches of economics, and areas of science.

Georg Wertheim, portrait by Emil Orlik, 1930

Worlds of Goods

Jewish businessmen active in the trade of goods and products were particularly innovative and willing to take risks. For the most part, they ran small retail trade businesses managed by the family, specializing primarily in the sale of textiles, shoes, foodstuffs, and luxury food items. Now, they adapted their businesses to changing conditions by expanding their product range, opening extra branches, or by discovering new forms of distribution such as mail-ordering or the department store. Like many others, Georg Wertheim (1857–1939) made use of the possibilities provided by the path of consumer society. After completing their apprenticeships, he and his brothers began working in the small shop belonging to their parents, Abraham and Ida Wertheim in Stralsund. There being no storage space in the small shop, which initially consisted of no more than a room in their parents' apartment, the products they acquired from relatives at reasonable prices had to be sold

immediately. The profit margin was calculated so low that it could only be balanced by a large turnover. They therefore fixed prices rather than negotiating individually with customers, as was previously the custom. Another business principle they did away with was the customer's obligation to buy.

The Wertheim family succeeded in establishing their business. First they moved to larger premises, and shortly afterwards opened a branch in Rostock. Georg Wertheim opened the first Berlin branch at Moritzplatz in 1890; four years later, his first department store was built, introducing a new type of edifice emulated by all those coming after it. With its magnificent atrium and expansive flights of stairs, the Wertheim department store, designed by Alfred Messel and built in 1897/98 in Leipziger

Gloves and receipts from the Wertheim department store

Wertheim

Like cascading colors in a fountain of light,
Silken and brocaded ribbons of fabric fall
In heaps, awaiting some calicofantastic
Ball, and curl, gracily, in looping arabesques.

The lady speaks: this fabric is extraordin'ry.
A thousand salesmen bow down to the floor and then
Stand at attention, obsequiously smiling.
The lady speaks: I'll come again, perhaps—

KARL SCHÖNBERG

Strasse, became a symbol of modern Berlin. With their chic décor and attractive product presentation, the majority of these new "temples of consumerism," as well as the largest, arose for the most part in Berlin, but also in Munich, Nuremberg, Chemnitz or Düsseldorf, and were connected with the names Wertheim, Herman Tietz, and later Salman Schocken. Adolf Jandorf's "Kaufhaus des Westens" (KaDeWe), which opened in 1907 and remains legendary to this day, was the largest and most elegant department store in Germany at that time. With the KaDeWe, the dawning consumerist society erected its own monument.

Photograph of an unknown woman from the Instant-Photo-Automat at Wertheim's, Berlin, ca. 1925

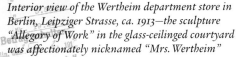

Interior view of the Wertheim department store in Berlin, Leipziger Strasse, ca. 1913—the sculpture "Allegory of Work" in the glass-ceilinged courtyard was affectionately nicknamed "Mrs. Wertheim"

"A country opens itself to modern business practices, a network of railroad tracks is laid, a revolutionary discovery is applied to a practical use ... How few understand that all this is the result not only of technical innovation, organizational talent, human labor and political support, but also of a creative and systematic financial spirit."

CARL FÜRSTENBERG (1850–1933)

Entrepreneurial Initiative

Jewish businessmen were the pioneers of modernism in transport businesses with greater capital, as well. In 1870, Wilhelm Kunstmann founded Prussia's largest shipping company in Stettin; Eduard Arnhold supplied Berlin with coal from Upper Silesia with his fleet of coal tugboats; and, as managing director of Hapag, the Hamburg-America Parcel Transportation, Albert Ballin (1857–1918) turned the business into the largest shipping company of the world. The ships of the most important transatlantic line transported millions of emigrants overseas. Ballin, son of a simple emigration agent, seized the chance offered by the migration business. His recipe for success consisted in the careful deliberation of trade politics and an openness to technical innovation. As one of the few so-called emperor's Jews, he advised Wilhelm II on economic matters.

Undoubtedly, the most prominent Jewish professional group was formed by the bankers, who, in response to a growing need for financing, assumed a central role in the context of the industrialization process. The significance and influence of the private banks was steadily diminishing. Whereas in the 19th century a banker of the stature of Gerson von Bleichröder (1822–1893) played an economically and politically important role as financier to Bismarck and the German Empire, corporations with an immense capital yield were now stepping into the foreground as players in the construction of a modern economy. Here, too, Jewish personalities were closely involved as founding fathers and leading

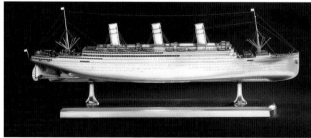

Model for the Express Liner "Imperator," 1912
left: Albert Ballin and the German Emperor Wilhelm II, ca. 1914

Emil Rathenau at his writing desk, ca. 1910

(1838–1915) wanted to improve people's living standards and bathe the city in bright light. Rathenau had recognized "humanity's insatiable hunger for electricity" early on and procured the German license on Thomas Alva Edison's patents in 1881. He founded the Deutsche Edison Gesellschaft or DEG (German Edison Company) and built Germany's first public power plant in Markgrafenstrasse in Berlin. A decisive step was thereby taken in 1885 towards an electrical energy supply for the whole of Germany. The personal risk was high, but Rathenau had made the right business decision: the DEG renamed itself the Allgemeine Elektrizitäts-gesellschaft or AEG (General Electricity Company) in 1887, and quickly grew into a large corporation represented in all fields of electrical engineering and developing new branches of industry. When Emil Rathenau died in 1915, his son Walther, soon to become foreign minister of the Weimar Republic, took over the direction of the enterprise.

employees. Thus, the Dresdner Bank emerged from the Jewish private bank Michael Kaskel in 1872. The former owners, Carl and Felix von Kaskel, were persuaded along with thirteen other bankers and investors by Eugen Gutmann (1840–1925) to form a stock corporation. Gutmann, after whom the new central bank building on Pariser Platz in Berlin is named, became the executive director of Dresdner Bank and remained affiliated with it until 1920. As one of the first bank managers in Germany, Gutmann pushed for the founding of multiple branches and developed the individual customer business: "Even the smallest of officials, and indeed every maid, has to have a deposit account."

Financed by the Berliner Handels-gesellschaft, a joint-stock bank with Jewish banker Carl Fürstenberg as its director, Emil Rathenau

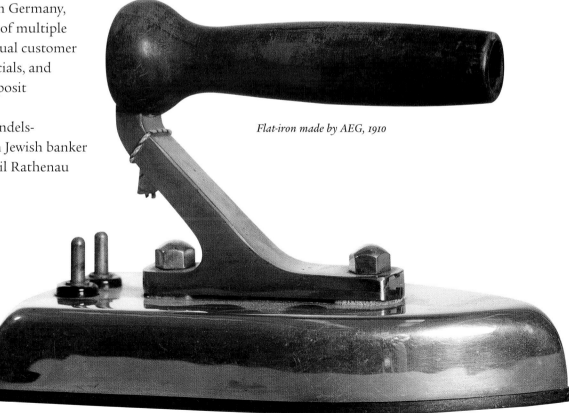

Flat-iron made by AEG, 1910

$$\frac{\varepsilon}{c^2} = \frac{m\,c^2}{\sqrt{1 - \frac{q^2}{c^2}}} \qquad (28)$$

> ## "Quests succeed only when passion insists."
>
> ALBERT EINSTEIN

Science

The largest attraction for the younger generation of German Jews, however, was undoubtedly radiated by the academic professions, and in the years around the turn of the century, the percentage they comprised rose more rapidly than in any other professional area. It was precisely the economic success of their parents' generation that enabled many young Jews to graduate from university. Many of them no longer wanted to follow in the footsteps of their fathers, but strove instead for the intellectual and artistic professions in the areas of science, media and culture.

Because the prospects here remained limited despite formal equality—state positions as teachers, professors or judges were hardly attainable due to the anti-Semitism still prevailing—most Jewish academics strove for the so-called free professions, becoming lawyers, notaries, doctors or veterinarians. Even those who made it as far as a university career, such as Leo Arons (1860–1919), the physicist and inventor of the neon light, had to take intrigues and possible dismissal into account. In Arons' case, also a member of the SPD and one of the leaders of the union movement, the emperor gave personal orders to the Prussian ministry of culture to "immediately remove" the private Berlin instructor "from the university and his position." And so it was; Arons, who had studied together with Walther Rathenau in Strasbourg, later found a position in Rathenau's AEG.

Thus, the majority of Jewish students prepared themselves for later independence from the very beginning; this explains, among other things, a concentration on medical studies. Later, the ratio shifted in favor of law and the humanities. The medical profession held a long tradition among Jews, and many Jewish doctors enjoyed recognition as researchers and pioneers—such as Paul Ehrlich (1854–1915), the Nobel Prize winner in medicine on whose research chemotherapy was based, or Magnus Hirschfeld (1868–1935), the founder of sexual science.

Jewish researchers became prominent in other scientific areas, as well; like Ehrlich and Hirschfeld, they did not, for the most part, hold a university professorship, but were active in specialized clinics or research centers, the most important of which was the Kaiser Wilhelm Society—known today as the Max Planck Institute. Fritz Haber (1868–1934), who together with Carl Bosch received the Nobel Prize for chemistry in 1918, researched here, and Albert Einstein (1879–1955) found excellent working conditions at a Kaiser Wilhelm Institute. Along with their pioneering discoveries, it was precisely Haber and Einstein who in very different ways illuminate the two faces of research: while Einstein appealed to the scientist's morals and sense of responsibility, Haber's behavior in World War I demonstrated the necessity of such an appeal. The awarding of the Nobel Prize to Haber and Bosch was highly controversial. The prize winners were

Paul Ehrlich in his study, ca. 1910

honored for the synthesis of ammonia, a procedure which not only enables the manufacture of nitrogen fertilizer, but also the manufacture of explosives. The patriot Haber placed himself and his research in the service of the military and went on to become the father of modern chemical warfare.

Media, Art, and Culture

That a public controversy followed upon Haber's being awarded the Nobel Prize, that such a debate could even constitute a "public," was due more than anything else to the media, which from 1900 on

above left: Excerpt from Albert Einstein's manuscript for "The Theory of Special Relativity," 1912

left: Fritz Haber with soldiers and the one-millionth gas shell, ca. 1915

underlay: Institute for the Science of Sexuality, Berlin-Tiergarten, 1920

"I am going to found a journal, 'The Wild Jews'— a poltical-artistic journal. I'll write a letter to Karl Kraus, something like this, listen: 'Won't you print my Journal of the Wild Jews along with yours, sort of on the sly? The Fackel won't feel a thing, and then I'd have a living. Your devout admirer, Jussuf, Prince.' What do you think, Franz dear, would he do it?"

ELSE LASKER-SCHÜLER
to Franz Marc, 1913

Rudolf Mosse,
portrait by Franz von Lenbach, 1898

developed swiftly. Especially in Berlin, Rudolf Mosse (1843–1920) and Leopold Ullstein (1826–1899) along with his sons had expanded their publishing houses into influential news corporations. The national organization of the advertising business placed the newspapers' self-financing on firm footing; when permission for street sales of newspapers, previously strictly subscription material, was granted in 1904, a mass press arose which turned the newspaper city Berlin into the cultural center of the country. Papers which were already popular, such as Ullstein's *Berliner Morgenpost* or Mosse's *Berliner Tageblatt* (from 1872), experienced an edition explosion; moreover, with the *BZ am Mittag* (from 1904), the "fastest newspaper of the world," or the *8-Uhr-Abendblatt* (from 1910), a format was developed combining regular news coverage, headlines and press photos: the 'tabloid press' which hit the nerve of a mass audience. In the new field of photo journalism from 1930 onwards, young female photographers increasingly had their break-through—Lotte Jacobi, Yva, Aenne Biermann.

Information and enlightenment, however, held priority over simple edification or entertainment. For Mosse, the newspaper should be "an advisor and fellow striver aiming to pave the way— sometimes rousing, sometimes warning and reserved, sometimes determining and sometimes in opposition." Many Jewish journalists and publicists adopted a "civilizatory" aim of this kind. Exemplary for the liberal, independent spirit of the time was the legendary editor-in-chief of the *Berliner Tageblatt*, Theodor Wolff (1868–1943), after whom one of today's most prestigious journalist's prizes is named and whose editorials—alongside the essays, commentaries, and criticism of Alfred Kerr, Julius Bab, Maximilian Harden or Ernst Feder—found national acclaim.

Advertisement for the Berliner Tageblatt, ca. 1905

Between 1890 and 1933, a magazine culture
developed which would have been unthinkable without the names of Max Osborn, Siegfried Jacobsohn,
Willy Haas and Paul Westheim. In Herwarth
Walden's (1878–1941) artists' forum *Der Sturm,* poems
by Else Lasker-Schüler appeared alongside etchings
by Oskar Kokoschka, short stories by Alfred Döblin
next to graphic works by the Russian avant-garde.
From the combination of word and art, a multi-
layered artistic network emerged.

Painters such as Max Liebermann and Lesser
Ury helped modernism in Germany onto the road to
success. Through Ludwig Meidner and Jacob Steinhardt, Otto Freundlich and Felix Nussbaum, Jewish
artists were a constant part of the subsequent art
trends in the early 20th century, as well, testing new
perspectives and forms of interpretation. Paul
Cassirer, Herwarth Walden or Alfred Flechtheim
were the gallerists who exhibited and established
the art of the European avant-garde—successfully,
but always at high risk and in the face of hostility.

Max Lieberman,
Self-Portrait with Straw Hat, 1929

Ludwig Meidner,
Self-Portrait at the Easel, 1912

*left: Max Reinhardt,
ca. 1925*

*right: Otto Brahm
in his loge at the
Deutsches Theater,
painting by Lesser Ury,
1901*

From early modernism to the "Neues Bauen" or "New Building" of the twenties, Otto Kaufmann and Erich Mendelsohn counted as excellent representatives of their field.

Theater people such as Otto Brahm and Max Reinhardt mirrored society on the stage with their contemporary dramas. Reinhardt (1873–1943), co-founder of the Salzburger Festspiele and, until 1933, director of the Deutsches Theater and the Kammerspiele in Berlin, is considered to be a pioneer of modern theater. With his musically animated mass scenes, he bewitched public and critics alike. In the words of Gerhart Hauptmann, he applied a new style "to the entire substance of German theater in masterful freedom." Composers such as the founder of twelve-tone music, Arnold Schoenberg, polarized the public with their works, while at the same time sensitizing it to new artistic dimensions.

While Jewish artists played a decisive role in the aesthetic production of modernism, this was equally true for the mediation and dissemination of contemporary culture on the part of publishers, publicists and critics. Publisher Samuel Fischer (1859–1934) acquainted the German reader with modern German and world literature. Kurt Wolff (1887–1963) turned his house into the most important forum for young expressionists such as Carl Einstein and published writers such as Max Brod, Franz Kafka or Franz Werfel.

Art historians of a younger Jewish generation, such as Richard Krautheimer or Erwin Panofsky, supported the literary and artistic criticism of the time. Often prevented from pursuing an academic career, critical minds from philosophy and sociology presented fundamental works of analysis and reflection on developments in society. Georg Simmel with his "Philosophie des Geldes" (Philosophy of Money, 1900), Siegfried Kracauer with his study

*Walter Benjamin's "Einbahnstraße"
(One-Way Street): jacket montage by
Sasha Stone; Rowohlt, Berlin, 1928*

on "Die Angestellten" (The Employees, 1930), and
Walter Benjamin with his collection of short prose
and aphorisms "Einbahnstraße" (One-Way Street,
1928) appear as pioneers of a theory of modernism.

"From our great city the shout reverberates,
the din of technology; the fear of death bears a warning face behind made-up, empty masks, the desire,
however, reaches for the moon," thus Else Lasker-
Schüler (1876–1945) in her prose collection "Concert"
describes the tension of the era and the magnetic
pull of the city: "Our city Berlin is strong and terrible, and her wings know to where they want to fly.
That's why the artist returns, yes, always returns, to
Berlin, for here art's clock beats with the pulse of
the time."

*Fritzi Massary in the operetta
"A Woman Who Knows What She
Wants," in the Metropol-Theater, Berlin,
1932, and with Oskar Strauss at a
rehearsal for "A Woman Who Knows
What She Wants"*

"In everything we do, we are seeking to
ensure the continuity of our selves; we pick
up pen and chisel for the sole purpose of
lending longevity to the moment; no
deluge should ensue after us; we wish not
to be the last of our kind; we love the
future generations that we carry within us,
and they should follow in our tracks."

GEORG HERMANN (1871–1943)
Sehnsucht

Tradition and Change— Shabbat

The Shabbat is the day of rest in the Jewish week, and at the same time the highest holy day in Judaism. Its existence is founded in three events that are related in the Torah, its origin formed by the story of creation at the beginning of the first book of Moses. After six days of creating the world, God rested on the seventh day. The Shabbat also commemorates the exodus out of Egypt. A fundamental and significant institution, the Shabbat commandment comprises one of the ten commandments given by God to the Israelites on Mount Sinai.

What is Done on the Jewish Day of Rest?

To rest means to do no work of any kind, to create nothing new, and to make no changes to the world. Jews believe that the world is in a special, holy state on the Shabbat, that it stands still for twenty-five hours. The rabbis make a distinction in the Torah between thirty-nine main works carried out during the building of the tabernacle on Mount Sinai and which are forbidden on the Shabbat. All other proscriptions are derived from these. The more well-known refer to cooking and baking, and, in recent times, to the turning on and off of electrical appliances.

All work has to be completed before the Shabbat begins. Friday is the day on which the holy day is thoroughly prepared for. The apartment is cleaned, an abundant meal is cooked, the table is ceremoniously prepared. Shortly before sundown, the woman of the house lights the two Shabbat candles and pronounces the blessing. Then the Shabbat begins, and the family might go to synagogue to celebrate the *Kabbalat Shabbat*, where the Shabbat is received as a bride or queen in traditional songs and prayers.

Shabbat oven, The Netherlands,
early 19th century

The Kiddush Ceremony

At home, the children are blessed and the Shabbat ceremony begins with the *Kiddush* or sanctification. Thanks are given to God the creator, who provides the wine and bread which symbolize daily sustenance, thus sanctifying the activity of drinking and eating. Following the blessing over the wine, all participants wash their hands. Afterwards, the blessing is pronounced over the two loaves of braided bread, known as hallah or barhes, lying on the table, covered by a cloth. After each blessing, everyone present drinks from the wine and eats a piece of bread, whereby the Kiddush takes on an integrative meaning by drawing the family together. Afterwards, the ceremonious meal begins.

Havdalah set by Yaacov Greenvurcel, silver and wood, Jerusalem, 2001

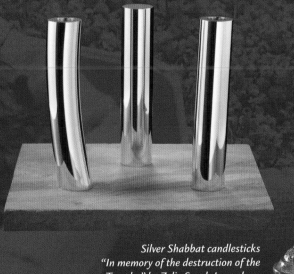

Silver Shabbat candlesticks "In memory of the destruction of the Temple," by Zelig Segal, Jerusalem, 1998–2001

right: Spice box, silver-plated brass, from the Württembergische Metallwarenfabrik, Geislingen an der Steige, ca. 1890–1910

"A Good Week"

There is also a special ceremony for the close of the Shabbat, the *Havdalah*, meaning separation, differentiation. On Saturday evening after sundown, twenty-five hours after its beginning, the Shabbat ends. A chalice of wine filled to the brim stands for the abundance of the Shabbat and the divine blessing.

A candle woven from several strands is lit. The aroma of spices from the *besamin box*—cloves, cinnamon and nutmeg blossoms—alleviates the departure of the Shabbat. After the pronouncement of the Havdalah blessing, the candle is extinguished with the wine. The Shabbat ends with the extinction of the flame, the faithful wish each other "shavua tov" ("a good week"), and can turn on the lights once again and resume their customary activities.

From the Ghetto to Zion—this print by Ephraim Moses Lilien
decorated the official postcard for the Fifth Zionist Conference in Basel 1901.
Detail from a circular distributed by the Jewish National Fund,
Cologne, 1907.

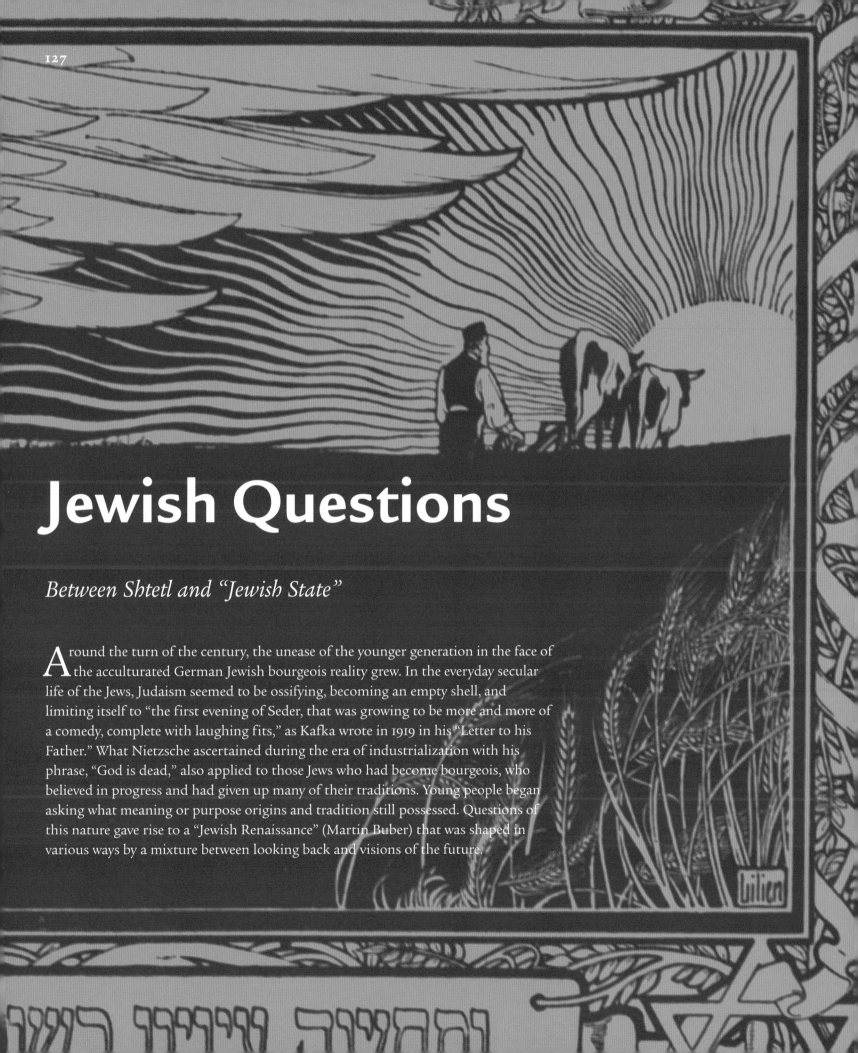

Jewish Questions

Between Shtetl and "Jewish State"

Around the turn of the century, the unease of the younger generation in the face of the acculturated German Jewish bourgeois reality grew. In the everyday secular life of the Jews, Judaism seemed to be ossifying, becoming an empty shell, and limiting itself to "the first evening of Seder, that was growing to be more and more of a comedy, complete with laughing fits," as Kafka wrote in 1919 in his "Letter to his Father." What Nietzsche ascertained during the era of industrialization with his phrase, "God is dead," also applied to those Jews who had become bourgeois, who believed in progress and had given up many of their traditions. Young people began asking what meaning or purpose origins and tradition still possessed. Questions of this nature gave rise to a "Jewish Renaissance" (Martin Buber) that was shaped in various ways by a mixture between looking back and visions of the future.

The personal history of Franz Rosenzweig (1886–1929) provides an example for this inner conflict and search for identity. Rosenzweig, who came from a respected, acculturated family in Kassel, was on the verge of converting to Christianity, as some of his friends and relatives had already done. Before taking this step, however, he wanted to get to know the religion he was about to give up. His intensive studies carried him back to his Jewish roots, and Rosenzweig went on to become one of modern Judaism's most profound thinkers. In his major work, "Der Stern der Erlösung" (The Star of Redemption), written during World War I, he attempted to uncover the buried Jewish sense of self and to reconsider its relationship to Christianity—both Jews and Christians ought to identify with the positive content of their tradition once again.

The Zionist Movement

When Czar Alexander II was assassinated and Russia subsequently plunged into a crisis, the Jewish world was shattered. If the hope had still existed that the western model of emancipation would ultimately prevail in Russia, as well, these hopes were cruelly disappointed. The Russian state not only did nothing to prevent the flare-up of anti-Semitism; it accepted and supported it, which led to the worst cases of persecution since the Cossack pogroms. As early as 1882, following the first pogrom in Odessa, an essay appeared in Berlin which attracted considerable attention: "Auto-emancipation! Warning by a Russian Jew to fellow members of his race." Leon Pinsker (1821–1891), a young doctor from Odessa, took bitter stock therein: "The Jewish people has no fatherland of its own, although it has many motherlands; it has no center, no concentration, no government of its own, no representation. It is present everywhere and at home nowhere." Freedom and security for the Jews could only be guaranteed in "a country of our own." Where this "own country" should be was still open in the early days of the movement, but the millennia-old religious connection to destroyed Jerusalem soon led to the association of the Jewish national idea with a return to *Zion*. The longing for Zion was as old as the Diaspora. In the Hebrew Bible, the term "Zion" initially refers to the Jebusite fortress in Jerusalem, renamed "City of David" following its conquest by King David. As the city grew, the term "Zion" soon came to include the Temple Mount and its shrine; later, it became synonymous for all of Palestine. Various political expectations were linked to this

*After the Pogrom,
painting by Maurice Minkowski,
ca. 1910*

*underlay: Postcard sent
by Franz Rosenzweig while on
active service in the army,
with a part of the manuscript
for "The Star of Redemption,"
1918*

"We try to run our household strictly in accordance with the kashrut laws, so that any Jew, even the most orthodox, can eat with us. But I want to have the freedom for myself to eat with any friend who happens not to be Jewish."

EDITH SCHEINEMANN-ROSENZWEIG, NÉE HAHN (1895–1979)
the wife and collaborator of Franz Rosenzweig

"own country." The idea of a socialist community free from outside rule mingled with conceptions of territoriality and the national state. Yet it was not until Theodor Herzl (1860–1904) that a charismatic personality appeared who was able to turn an idea into an international movement, to gather public attention and to direct political energy to the establishment of a "Jewish State." Herzl was born the son of a businessman in Budapest; as the Paris correspondent for the Viennese newspaper *Neue Freie Presse,* he reported on the trial against the captain Alfred Dreyfus that had caused a sensation all over Europe as a scandal of justice with anti-Semitic motives. During the course of the so-called Dreyfus Affair, Herzl had come to the conclusion that the Jews were a nation united by a common enemy and would only be able to realize their right to self-determination in a state of their own. When his book "The Jewish State" appeared in the spring of 1896, in which he elevated the Jewish question to a "global issue ... to be regulated on the counsel of civilized peoples," he spoke to the hearts of all those who were disappointed by the decline of bourgeois, liberal values.

At the first Zionist Congress in Basel only one year later, 196 delegates from 16 countries announced that "*Zionism* strives on behalf of the

*Carpet showing
Theodor Herzl with Jerusalem's
Tower of David in the background,
1920*

*Theodor Herzl, portrait by
Hermann Struck, 1903*

Label for the wine "Chateau Queen of Sheba," Société Coopérative Vigneronne des Grandes Caves, Richon-le-Zion & Zichron-Jacob Ltd. in Palestine, 1920s

Jewish people for the creation of a legally secure homeland in Palestine." At the same time, the six-pointed star, the Magen David, literally "Shield of David," was chosen as the symbol of the movement. At first, Theodor Herzl limited himself to his journal in expressing his satisfaction over the outcome of the congress: "In Basel, I founded the Jewish state. If I said that out loud today, it would meet with universal laughter. Perhaps in five years, certainly in fifty, everyone will understand it."

The program was soon followed by concrete steps. At the fifth Zionist Congress in 1901, which took place once again in Basel, the Jewish National Fund (JNF) was founded. The JNF issued shares and collected donations; these financial resources were to be used to purchase land in Palestine from 1907 on. The *halutzim* or young pioneers, who placed themselves and their physical strength in the service of building the aspiring homeland, became the ideal Zionist image and symbol of national Renaissance. In order to equip the youth for the *aliyah*, the migration to *Eretz Israel*, and at the same time to fight against the anti-Semitic, distorted image of the physically inferior Jew, numerous sports associations came into being in which children and young men

imitated the ideal of the "muscle Jew" propagated by Max Nordau.

It was at the fifth Zionist Congress, as well, that an inner-Zionist opposition came onto the scene for the first time, lamenting the movement's neglect of religious and cultural dimensions. The "Democratic Faction" centered around Martin Buber (1878–1965) and the artist Ephraim Moses Lilien (1874–1925) was not interested in division, but in constructive criticism. As a result, Lilien in particular helped lend Zionism a recognizable, unifying image, leading many supporters to identify with the movement's aims. Lilien designed an iconography for the Zionist movement by combining Jewish motifs with contemporary European Art Nouveau. Old Jewish men with long beards, heroic subjects from the holy scriptures, idealized portraits of the Holy Land, the sun rising over the pyramids with the word "Zion" blazing on it—Lilien selected images that were part of the symbolic language of political emancipatory movements at the time; the rising sun, for instance, had been in the regular repertoire of political imagery since the French Revolution.

Grape harvest in Rishon le Zion, Palestine, ca. 1925

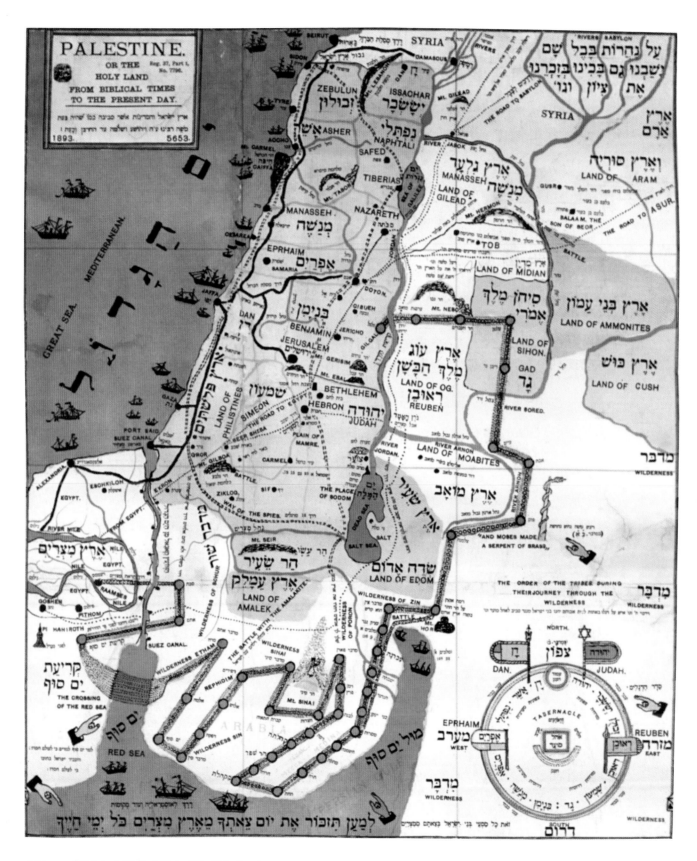

A New and Original Biblical Map of the Holy Land,
by Jacob Goldzweig, Haifa 1893

Eastern Jews

In order to escape economic misery and brutal persecution, well over one million Eastern European Jews fled their homeland between 1881 and 1914 for the West, most of them with America as their goal. Thus, Germany was a mere stopover on the journey abroad for the majority of the emigrants. A small number of Eastern Jews settled in Germany. The ever-increasing racist hostility towards Jews turned these immigrants into welcome scapegoats for resentment and instigation.

For German Jewish intellectuals, the contact with Eastern Jewry, especially with a stricter religious practice and *Hassidic* mysticism, proved to be a formative experience. During the Great War, the experiences of Jewish soldiers and correspondents on the eastern front in Poland and Russia forged a new

Postcard for the Festival of the Makkabi Athletic Association in Ostrava, 1929

ideal, as described by Sammy Gronemann (1875-1952) in his autobiographical report, "Hawdoloh und Zapfenstreich" (Havdalah and Curfew), on his activities as an interpreter for Yiddish.

Gronemann's depiction of the religious, communal life in Eastern Europe contributed considerably to the positive reassessment of Eastern Judaism. The lawyer, writer, and journalist wrote without pathos, yet with affectionate satire about the "chaos" that reigned in the synagogues between Kovno and Warsaw. "Fasting and mourning on days of repentance are halfway understood in the West as well, but the real joy, the joy in the teachings, in the law, is known only there," he reported on the debating, singing, and dancing in the prayer hall. "Why are all those people rejoicing? What, after all, is this Torah that they are celebrating? A law with innumerable commandments and prohibitions, that limits all life's pleasures and imposes high taxes! Is it conceivable that any European people would delight in a civil or penal code? Or fiscal law for that matter?" Gronemann summed up: "There in the East, one feels absolutely sure about what one is doing and one's assets, whereas in the West one constantly fears a bursting through the thin front—this synagogue has remained the center of Jewish will and Jewish power."

In contrast to the assimilated "Western Jewry," alienated from their traditions, the *shtetl* became a vision of an intact, authentic Jewish community living in self-confidence and dignity. This 'Eastern Jewish cult' took a socialist, utopian turn and was expressed in countless literary and artistic works. In Martin Buber's "Tales of the Hasidim," or Joseph Roth's book "Wandering Jews," the "superficial" world of the German Jews is contrasted with the genuine religiosity and spirituality of the Eastern Jews: "Jewish Jews," according to the central message, could only be found in the East. In his "Travels to Poland," Alfred

Döblin for instance writes that he had long believed "that what he saw in Germany, the industrious people, the alert intellectuals, the countless uncertain, unhappy, fine people, were the Jews. Now I see: they are uprooted specimens, far away from the core of the people that lives and subsists here."

Such a vision also gave wing to the imagination of Jewish artists, such as Lilien, Joseph Budko, Ludwig Meidner, or Uriel Birnbaum. The etchings and lithographs of Hermann Struck (1876–1944) that illustrate Arnold Zweig's book "Das ostjüdische Antlitz" (The Eastern Jewish Countenance, 1919), for instance, lend a concise, aesthetic expression to the author's pathos. As he himself testified, the expressionist Jakob Steinhardt (1887–1968) created his religious ecstasy and apocalyptic vision based on his encounters with Eastern Jews: he believed that he could recognize his own ancestors in their faces.

The "Power of Synthesis"

The spectrum of positions was broad and manifold, and heated disputes erupted among their supporters. Sometimes the discussion was carried into the non-Jewish public realm as well. Zionists and anti-Zionists reproached one another mutually; whereas one group complained about the loss of Jewish substance through assimilation, the other chastised an exaggerated Jewish nationalism. The Central-

Verein deutscher Staatsbürger jüdischen Glaubens (Central Association of German Citizens of Jewish Faith) represented the liberal majority, whereas the Zionistische Vereinigung für Deutschland (Zionist Association for Germany) declared that membership in both associations was irreconcilable.

In the atmosphere of these discussions, the sociologist Werner Sombart's demonstration of support played an important role. In his essay "Die Zukunft der Juden" (The Future of the Jews), published in 1912, Sombart claimed that it was "in the interests of the soul of the German people" that Germany be liberated "from the clutches of the

On the Way to the Prayer-House,
painting by Jakob Steinhardt, 1921

Moses gazes upon the Promised Land,
painting by Lesser Ury, 1927–28

Two Women,
painting by Joseph Budko,
1925

Jewish spirit" should a Jewish state come into existence. When some of the Zionists took up Sombart's comments—tinged as they were with anti-Semitism—as confirmation of their demands, representatives of the German Jewish organizations felt attacked from within their own ranks. On February 5, 1914, they published a "declaration" with 300 signatures in all the important daily newspapers in which they vehemently distanced themselves from the Zionists. The philosopher Hermann Cohen (1842–1918), one of the most prominent of those who signed and an important representative of liberal German Jewry, refuted political Zionism. Cohen, however, also saw Eastern Jewish religiosity as the most important source of Judaism. Three months after the anti-Zionist "declaration," he embarked on a lecture tour in Russia against the backdrop of the ritual murder trial of Mendel Beilis in Kiev. His lectures, attended by thousands in St. Petersburg, Moscow, and other Russian cities, turned into demonstrations for solidarity with his request to mediate between both cultural worlds. Cohen planned to set up Jewish schools in Eastern Europe and establish the "Science of Judaism" in the East; the inception of World War I, however, put a stop to these plans.

Cohen, who compiled his fundamental meditations on Judaism in his late work "Religion der Vernunft aus den Quellen des Judentums" (Religion of Reason from the Sources of Judaism), published posthumously in 1919, had reservations about the confessionalizing of the religion. His historical and political hope consisted in the possibility that a cosmopolitan German identity could combine with messianic Judaism to form a fundamental factor in world peace. His pupil Franz Rosenzweig was also skeptical towards Zionism. Through turning to practical Jewish life, his concept of "new learning" helped the following generation find a new way out of the confusion of assimilation. With the Freies Jüdisches Lehrhaus (Free Jewish House of

Education), that he founded in 1920 in Frankfurt am Main, he wanted to lead "to life" through education, "from the periphery back to the center; from the outside to inside," to fill the gaps left by the loss of religious tradition.

In a letter in 1921 to Max Warburg, Rosenzweig's teacher and friend, Rabbi Anton Nehemia Nobel (1871–1922), described precisely this contradiction of German and Jewish identity that seemed unbridgeable to many as being a binding "strength": "There is no doubt in my mind that the history of Israel cannot only be evaluated religiously. At the same time it is the bearer of national development. I am rooted in this national Jewish world. But I also cannot imagine my life without Goethe, poet of the Germans. There is some sort of power of synthesis in me that binds and entwines both nationalisms. I know that they are both strong enough to withstand an alliance."

Hermann Cohen,
portrait by Max Liebermann,
1913

Eastern Jews in the Ruhr Valley

Still today, the Ruhr Valley is associated mainly with its industrial monuments, where heavy industry once prospered. It was one of the few regions in Germany, which has always been considered a country of emigration, that attracted migrants from both near and far. Hundreds of thousands of workers especially from Russia and Poland contributed significantly to the country's industrial growth. Some of those people were Jews.

*Segeroth, the immigrants'
quarter in Essen,
ca. 1900*

Transit through Germany

Between 1871 and the First World War, over five million people from Russia and the Austro-Hungarian empire left Europe via Bremen and Hamburg to escape the desolate economic conditions in their home countries. Brutal pogroms against the Jewish population, for instance in 1881 following the murder of Czar Alexander and in 1903 in Kishinev added to the pressure. This flow of migrants came to a halt in World War I and never reached the same scale again. The proportion of Jewish migrants is estimated at around 13 percent in 1880, rising to around 79 percent in 1906. Between 1903 and 1914, well over a million Jews emigrated from Russia. Only a very small proportion of the migrants actually settled in Germany.

Their transit through Germany to the ports of Bremen and Hamburg was organized by the two major shipping lines HAPAG and Lloyd, who transferred three-quarters of all emigrants in co-operation with the German authorities. Special trains took the people from specified border towns to collecting points, such as the transit railroad station at Berlin-Ruhleben. From these stations, which were equipped with disinfection centers and quarantine blocks, the emigrants were then transported to the North Sea ports.

In the Ruhr

It is difficult to say exactly how many Polish and Russian Jews lived in the industrial towns of the Ruhr Valley. Just after the First World War, about 4000 Jews worked down the coal mines. A great many were employed in heavy industry. The numbers were most certainly higher during the First World War as Jews were brought in, either voluntarily or by force, to replenish the declining labor force in Germany's industrial areas.

Many Jewish communities such as Duisburg, Dortmund, and Essen had a large number of foreign members following the First World War, which frequently led to conflicts. Eastern European Jews integrated themselves into already existing associations, but they also organized their own cultural societies, communal prayer groups, and groups to represent their political interests. They lived in the mass of tenement blocks that had mushroomed during industrialization, or in the old town centers with primitive facilities and no sanitation.

*"The free-loader,
or the recent immigrant,"
postcard ca. 1900*

"The newly arrived citizen"

History tells of a minority whose status was jeopardized twice over. Like all foreigners, Jews with Polish or Russian citizenship or even as "stateless persons" were permanently threatened with expulsion, a verdict that could be pronounced at any time through a change in regulations. Like all migrants, they were strangers who had to gain a new economic and social status in an unaccustomed environment. However, Jewish immigrants in particular were confronted with negative stereotypes that dominated the way they were viewed by the host society, by German Jews, the authorities, and the general public.

"The Eastern Jew" was seen as backward, loud, and ugly. The civil service's image of the "newly arrived citizen" was colored with anti-Semitic racism. The cliché implied that Eastern European Jews were socially deviant, diseased Jews who earned themselves quick fortunes by suspicious means.

A number of preconceived ideas still dominate even in today's search for traces of Eastern Jewish life in Germany. They are shaped by a romantic, picturesque view of life in the Polish shtetl which the "Eastern Jews" supposedly imported to Germany. It depicts a life firmly anchored in traditional culture and religion, poor but contented, accompanied by cheerful klezmer music. The lives of the workers in the industrial towns of the Ruhr Valley had very little in common with this.

The businessman Richard Stern wearing the highest German war-time decoration, the Iron Cross, in front of his store in Cologne during the boycott of Jewish institutions, April 1, 1933

"Awakened from the dream"

The Completion and Destruction of Emancipation

In his autobiography entitled "My Path as a German and a Jew," published in 1921, Jakob Wassermann (1873–1934) expressed the resigned observation that it was futile to live and die for "the people of poets and thinkers"; "they say: he is a Jew." With this statement, the writer was referring to a concrete disillusionment which he himself had experienced: only a few years earlier, thousands of German Jews had joined the war effort and died for their homeland, for Germany.

The outbreak of the Great War was embraced and celebrated by the majority of Germans. When Emperor Wilhelm II avowed in August 1914 in a burst of national exuberance: "I no longer know of any parties, I know of Germans only," the Jewish population took this to be a promise. They hoped that their patriotism and loyalty would refute anti-Semitism and finally overcome the deficiencies in emancipation still in existence. That very same day, the Central-Verein deutscher Staatsbürger jüdischen Glaubens (Central Association of German Citizens of Jewish Faith) made public a flaming appeal: "In this fateful hour, the fatherland calls its sons to the flag. It goes without saying that every German Jew is prepared to sacrifice his sweat and blood as duty calls for. Comrades in faith! We call upon you to dedicate your strength to the fatherland above and beyond the measure of duty." Similar declarations were issued by the Verband der deutschen Juden (Organization of German Jews) and the Zionistische Vereinigung für Deutschland (The Zionist Association for

Germany). German Jews were no different from their non-Jewish countrymen in terms of their patriotism; even Jews who had emigrated abroad and to Palestine were now returning to stand by their fatherland. Voices that spoke against the war were rare: Karl Kraus, Sigmund Freud or Theodor Wolff, who regarded the prevailing enthusiasm over the war as a deviation from reason and humanism, remained lonely pariahs.

The Spirit of 1914

"I'm looking forward to the war." With these words, for instance, the forty year-old Social Democratic Reichstag delegate and lawyer Ludwig Frank (1874–1914), whose age-group in all likelihood would no longer have been enlisted, voluntarily joined the battle. One of the reasons he decided to serve was to help dismantle the mistrust of Jews and to further their social and political integration. He was to survive the war a mere three days. Transferred to the front on August 31, he fell on September 3, 1914, southeast of Lunéville in Lorraine—one of more than 12,000 German Jewish soldiers who died in the First World War.

Others, such as the lawyer Julius Fliess (1876–1955), were severely wounded. Fliess, who was already thirty-eight years old, had also volunteered with great enthusiasm immediately following mobilization. Blinded on the right side as a result of a bullet wound to the head, he was no longer classified as "capable of being used for war," yet he reported to the front again and again. He was not only promoted to lieutenant for his service, but honored with every military distinction, such as the Iron

*Mobilization 1914—
Fritz and Emma Schlesinger bid
the cavalryman Ludwig Börnstein
farewell on the avenue
Unter den Linden in Berlin*

Cross of the first and second class, the Silver Badge awarded to a wounded soldier akin to the Purple Heart, the Cross of Honor for front-line soldiers, the Hessian Badge of Military Honor, and the Austrian Cross for Distinguished Military Service, as well as numerous others. Yet the hopes for full recognition were soon disappointed. The longer the war dragged on, the more the "Spirit of 1914" evaporated. Frustration and continuing resentment nourished anti-Semitic attacks. The accusation for instance that Jews were shirking their military duty and front service served as a pretext for a "Jewish census" with the German military. Disguised as a confessional statistic, the war ministry ordered the registration of all those Jews subject to military service on October 11, 1916. It was felt to be a deep humiliation by the Jewish population as a whole and especially by those fighting on the front. Disillusionment and anger spread. The Central-Verein, which had always taken care to keep a balance, declared in 1918 that it was time to relinquish moderation and to "revert to attack," whereas the Zionist newspaper *Ost und West* (East and West), prophetically announced "that we have to prepare ourselves for a Jewish war when this war is over."

"Never, so our Emperor said in his call to arms to the German people, has Germany been beaten, if she was united. And united we were."

EUGEN FUCHS (1856–1923)
Lawyer and co-founder of the Central Association for German Citizens of Jewish Faith, on the outbreak of World War I

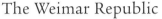

The Weimar Republic

When the weapons were silent after four years of war, the proclamation of the republic offered new hope. And indeed, after the monarchy was replaced with a democracy, the emancipation of the German Jews was complete.

The Weimar constitution, passed on July 31, 1919, did away with the last remaining restrictions on political integration. Paragraphs 109 and 128 prohibited the discrimination in public service due to religious reasons; Article 136 confirmed the independence of civil rights from religious persuasion, which had already been established in 1871: "Civil rights and duties are to be neither influenced nor limited by the practice of religious freedom. The enjoyment of civil rights as well as the admission to public office are independent of religious persua-

Honorary orders and decorations of Julius Fliess from World War I, 1914–18

sion. No one shall be called upon to reveal their religious faith." Furthermore, Jewish communities were now finally recognized as bodies of public law. Theoretically, German Jews were now no longer barred from any area of society—complete civil equality had finally been attained.

This new constitutional framework was now used and implemented by many German Jews representing their interests in public. The emancipation success, however, had to be converted into a political daily life colored by a continuing anti-Semitic undertone. Right-wing parties and associations, such as the Deutschvölkische Schutz- und Trutzbund (Defense Alliance of the German People) or the Nationalsozialistische Deutsche Arbeiterpartei (National Socialist German Workers' Party, NSDAP) systematically stirred up existing resentment. In large portions of the press, Jewish citizens were made responsible for nearly every symptom of crisis: they and other "traitors of the fatherland" had stabbed the long-victorious German army in the back and were now, as major capitalists, profiting from the defeat to boot.

The Social Democratic Reichstag delegate Julius Moses (1868–1942) was actively involved in the parliamentary investigative committee on the actual causes of the collapse of 1918. As a referee on the question of the German Reichstag's behavior during the Great War, he also clearly repudiated the legend of alleged "malingering" and in 1929 exposed the promotion of an anti-Semitic paper by the Notgemeinschaft Deutscher Wissenschaften (Emergency Association of German Sciences)—a precursor to the Deutsche Forschungsgemeinschaft (German Research Association). Moses, a convincing and quick-witted orator, counted among the numerous

members of parliament with Jewish backgrounds who had played key roles in the restructuring of society and the establishment of democratic structures since the inception of the Weimar Republic. As the SPD faction's speaker on health politics, the practicing doctor, who had been a member of the Reichstag throughout nearly the entire duration of the republic and who had also always been active as a representative of Jewish interests, was held in high non-partisan regard. In 1942, at the age of seventy-four, he was deported to Theresienstadt.

A Jew as Foreign Minister

The eventful history of the struggle over emancipation can be observed in the personal example of the entrepreneur, writer, and politician Walther Rathenau, whose career appeared to have fulfilled the hopes of the Jewish population. Born in 1867 as the son of the AEG founder Emil Rathenau and a member of the firm's board since 1899, Rathenau had established the department for military raw materials in the Prussian War Ministry during the First World War and was made Imperial Minister for Reconstruction in 1921. In January 1922, Rathenau, a member of the German Democratic Party (DDP), was appointed foreign minister of the Republic. Previously confronted with hostility due to his alleged "policy of appeasement" towards the victorious powers, he ultimately became the target of right-wing forces; in the National Socialist propaganda, he was considered to be the personification of the "Jewish Republic of Weimar."

"Shoot down Walther Rathenau—the goddamned Jewish pig"—the writing on the walls of Berlin's buildings soon met with tragic response: on June 24, 1922, not quite five months in office,

the foreign minister was shot in his car in Berlin's Königsallee. An investigation pointed to members of the radical right-wing organization Consul as culprits, who were connected to the Deutsch-völkische Schutz- und Trutzbund. In the aftermath, the Trutzbund was prohibited, and as a result, its 200,000 members in 530 local groups joined the NSDAP almost in their entirety.

The horror which the murder unleashed across party lines and in large parts of the population was great, yet the influence of German nationalist anti-democratic powers grew as well. While a coup d'état attempted by Adolf Hitler in conjunction with the "fatherland organizations" failed miserably in the year 1923, the German Nationalist People's Party (DNVP), was able to send ninety-six and the National Socialist Völkische Block thirty-two representatives to the Reichstag following the May elections of 1924. The situation remained for the

Biographical information sheet of Foreign Minister Dr. Walther Rathenau, Berlin, February 15, 1922. Under item 5, the inquiry about religious affiliation, he notes: "this question is unconstitutional."

left: Walther Rathenau, posthumous portrait by Emil Orlik, 1926

"To all front-line soldiers and Germans!"
Appeal for solidarity distributed by the former front-line fighter
Richard Stern, Cologne, end of March, 1933

most part stable until the stock market crash of 1929 and the ensuing economic crisis with its fear of social decline, in the aftermath of which anti-Semitic propaganda found a broad forum once again. The Central-Verein, with approximately 70,000 members in 1927 the largest Jewish organization of the Weimar Republic, tried in vain to ward off anti-Semitism through educational measures and publications such as the newspaper *C.V.-Zeitung*, which appeared on a weekly basis.

Destruction of Emancipation

In 1923, Hitler proclaimed that "The Jew is a race, but not human," making no secret of whom he was holding responsible for the country's social and economic problems. It must have been known to the majority of German voters, as well, who confirmed the "Führer" of the NSDAP in office on March 5, 1933 in free elections with 43.9 percent of the vote after he had been appointed chancellor to the Reich on January 30, 1933 by President Hindenburg.

Following Hitler's rise to power, the situation of the Jewish population in Germany immediately took a turn for the worse. The parties represented in the Reichstag—with the exception of the Social Democrats—cleared the way on March 23 to a dictatorship by empowering the new government to pass laws that did not comply with the constitution ("Ermächtigungsgesetz" or empowerment law). Hardly a month went by after the election before the first systematic act of violence occurred, demonstrating the disintegration of the constitutional state and the endangerment of Jews living in Germany. On Saturday, April 1, 1933, orders were given for a national boycott of Jewish establishments. Under the slogan "Germans, don't buy from Jews!,"

members of the National Socialist security forces SA and SS were posted in front of every Jewish store, lawyer's and doctor's office and barred anyone from entering, resulting in numerous violent occurrences. The explicit marking of Jewish stores and the explosion of anti-Semitic violence exerted immediate influence on the economic situation of above all Jewish retail traders who lost the majority of their non-Jewish customers and hence often the basis for their living. At the same time, the action revealed to German Jews their lack of rights and their defenselessness in a National Socialist state in the process of establishing itself.

Shortly afterwards, an even deeper turning point in German Jewish history was marked by the law passed on April 7, 1933 to "reinstate professional civil service," which rescinded every emancipation success achieved up until that point and which, for the first time since 1869, once again created a special legal status for Jews. Paragraph 3 of the law, the so-called Aryan paragraph, was regarded by the Reich's Minister of the Interior Frick as the "main item." Here, the legal criterion of citizenship was replaced by that of race, and from that point on the inhabitants of Germany were separated into "Aryans" and "Non-Aryans." This law, which excluded

National Socialist rule would soon come to an end, that it was a matter of getting through a short period of reduced circumstances under the protection of the public and abroad, which was due above all else to the economic crisis, this hope could not be held aloft for very long. "Like a horrible nightmare," the painter Max Liebermann (1847–1935) wrote in 1933, "the elimination of equality weighs upon us all, but especially upon the Jews, who, like myself, had given themselves over to the dream of assimilation… and as difficult as it has been for me, I have awakened from the dream that I have been dreaming throughout all of my long life."

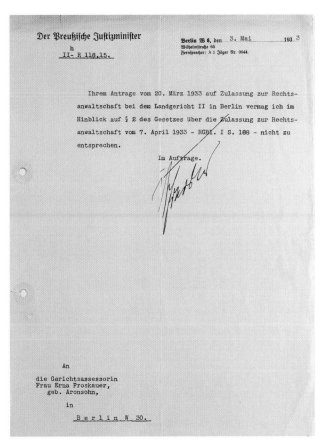

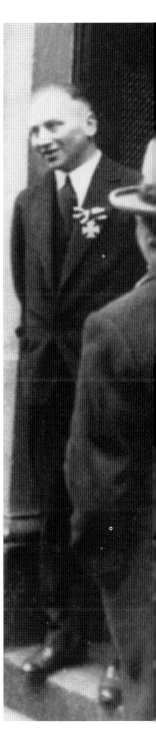

"Non-Aryans" from state service, became the model for the comprehensive anti-Jewish legislation of the National Socialists, which resulted in a multitude of increasingly minute decrees. As a result, university professors, lawyers, doctors, and officials lost their jobs for the sole reason of being Jewish. Equality of rights was nullified. While many—and many non-Jewish Germans, as well—initially believed that the

Rejection of Erna Proskauer's application for admission to the attorney's bar of the city of Berlin, May 3, 1933

left: The April Boycott—crowd assembled in front of the shoe store Leiser on the Tauentzienstrasse in Berlin, April 1, 1933

"Nesthäkchen and the Great War," Meidinger, Berlin, 1922

"Unforgettable days, these fantastic August days with the first triumphant advances of the German troops, the great self-sacrificing enthusiasm of the people at home! Those who were striving for the fatherland made their indelible mark on the souls of all young children for life."

Glowing with patriotism and the certainty of victory, Else Ury, the author of popular young adult novels, describes the first days of the Great War in her story "Nesthäkchen and the Great War," published in 1916 in the "Nesthäkchen" series.

Else Ury was born in 1877 into a tobacco merchant family in Berlin. As was customary for well-situated daughters in the Wilhelminian era, Else received no further education after leaving the high school for girls and remained in the family household. Like most of the acculturated Jewish minority, she saw herself as a German of Jewish faith. Under a pseudonym, she published poems and essays in the newspaper *Vossische Zeitung* before gaining recognition as a writer in 1906. The ten books of the "Nesthäkchen" series, which appeared between 1912/13 and 1925, were her greatest success and have sold almost seven million copies to date.

"Nesthäkchen" (little nestling) is the story of Annemarie Braun, the daughter of a Berlin physician. No matter how hard she tries, Annemarie is never perfect and her stories are filled with mishaps which she masters with lighthearted ease, thanks to her "carefree nature." The social milieu the author depicts and her subtle educational intentions clearly reflect Else Ury's own bourgeois family background. In contrast, though, to other popular contemporary writers of young adult literature, for instance Emmy von Rhoden with her "Trotzkopf" ("hothead") books, Else Ury integrated current political events into her stories.

Like many other Germans, both Jewish and non-Jewish, Else Ury welcomed the Great War and was actively involved in war relief work. This involvement and enthusiasm is reflected in the book "Nesthäkchen and the Great War." Annemarie is a keen member of the young women's relief association. The current of ultra-nationalism is evident in the episode about the

"Nesthäkchen" and Nationalism

so-called German Polish girl Vera, who is harassed by the heroine: "Anyone who talks with her... is a traitor to the fatherland." Only when Vera's father dies for Germany on the battlefront, does Annemarie change her attitude. Else Ury uses the war as an educational instrument: "Overwhelming love of the fatherland, un-bounded self-sacrifice for those out on the front. Uplifting pride in being a German boy or a German girl, and the resulting duty to fulfill their duty with excellence in this difficult time, despite their youth." These last sentences of the book reveal that the author was convinced there would be a "victorious peace"—as a loyal monarchist, the lost war must have seemed like a bitter defeat to her. In 1950, this particular volume was removed from the series.

From her royalties as a successful writer, Else Ury bought a country house in 1926 in her beloved mountain village of Krummhübel in the Riesengebirge. She named the house "Nesthäkchen." However, she was only able to enjoy her holiday home for a little over a decade: on December 3, 1938, the National Socialist regime ordered the confiscation of Jewish assets, and she was forced to sell her property. As a Jewish author, she had been expelled from the German National Association of Writers in 1935 and was banned from publishing any further books. By 1937, all her young adult novels had disappeared from the public libraries. Nevertheless, Ury's stories still remained popular. Despite the continuing loss of civil rights and increasing discrimination, she decided not to emigrate as she did not want to leave her ninety year-old mother behind on her own. Else Ury was deported to Auschwitz in January 1943.

Else Ury, ca. 1938

underlay:
The country house
"Nesthäkchen," ca. 1938

In the exhibition space of the Jewish Museum in Oranienburgerstrasse, Berlin, ca. 1935

The Jewish Museum opened on January 24, 1933, six days before the National Socialists assumed power. For the Jews, who were increasingly isolated socially as well as culturally, the Jewish Museum became an inspiring refuge. The museum was closed following the November Pogrom of 1938.

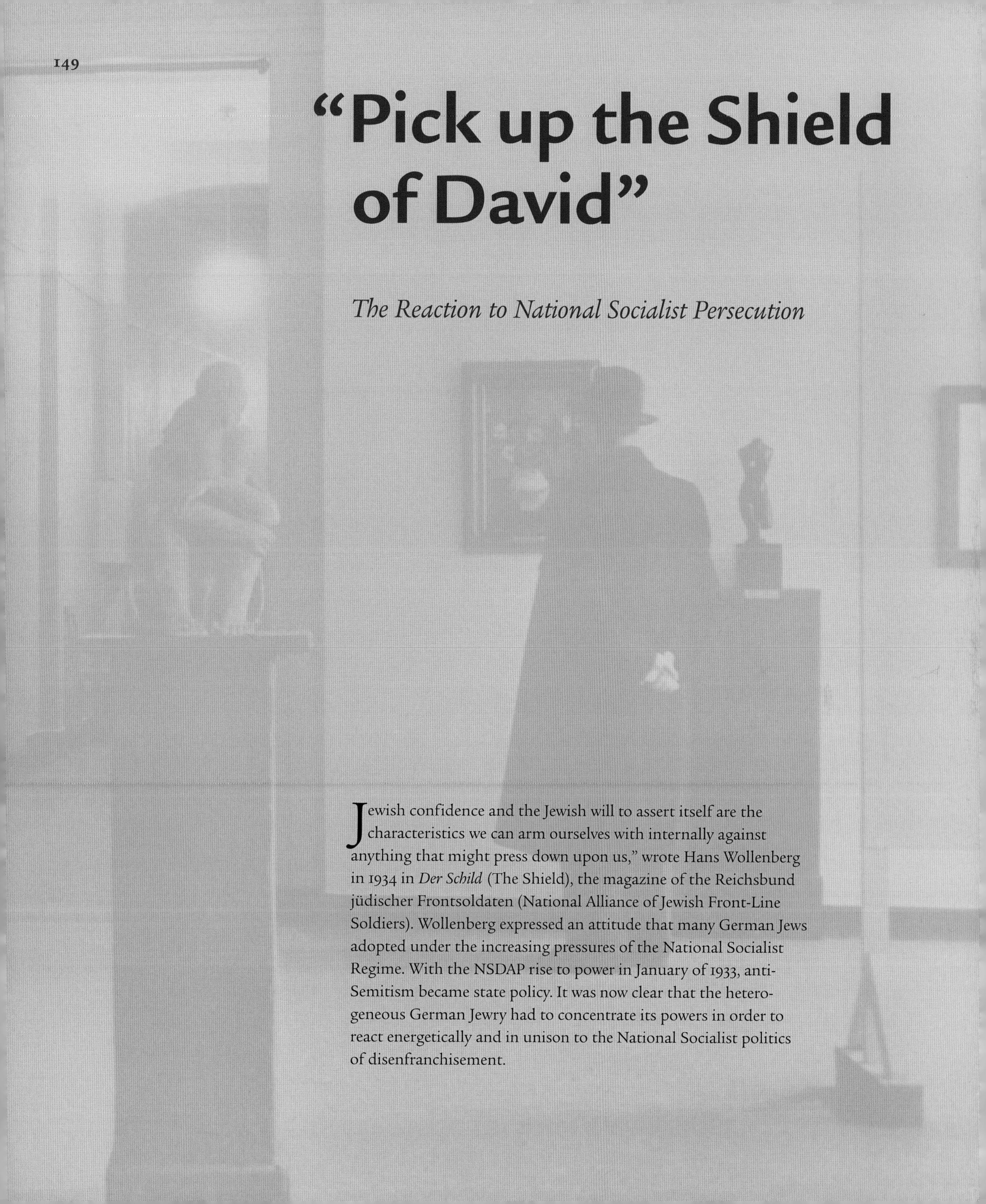

"Pick up the Shield of David"

The Reaction to National Socialist Persecution

Jewish confidence and the Jewish will to assert itself are the characteristics we can arm ourselves with internally against anything that might press down upon us," wrote Hans Wollenberg in 1934 in *Der Schild* (The Shield), the magazine of the Reichsbund jüdischer Frontsoldaten (National Alliance of Jewish Front-Line Soldiers). Wollenberg expressed an attitude that many German Jews adopted under the increasing pressures of the National Socialist Regime. With the NSDAP rise to power in January of 1933, anti-Semitism became state policy. It was now clear that the hetero-geneous German Jewry had to concentrate its powers in order to react energetically and in unison to the National Socialist politics of disenfranchisement.

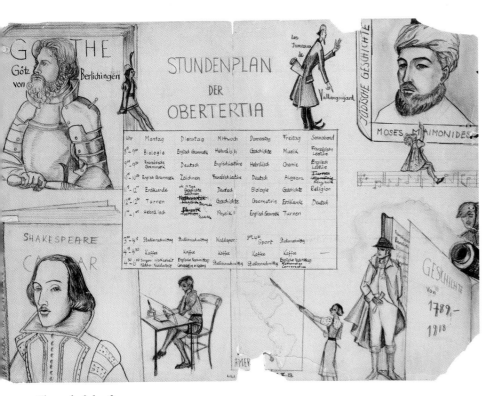

Class schedule of Lilly Cassel, student at the private Jewish Kaliski School in Berlin-Grunewald, 1938

Under the leadership of the well-known rabbi Leo Baeck (1873–1956), the first organization for all Jewish Germans, approximately 560,000 in number, was formed on September 17, 1933: the Reichsvertretung der deutschen Juden (National Representation of German Jews). Along with the representation of Jewish interests in dealings with the Nazi state and the strengthening of the inner cohesion of Jewry, its primary task consisted in setting up a comprehensive self-help network. A central charity post collected money from members of the community in order to balance the effects of the repression and of the "Law to Reestablish Civil Servants" from April 7, 1933, as well as to alleviate the deprivation resulting from unemployment and professional ruin. Beyond this, a Jewish school and health system was established in which teachers and doctors who had lost their jobs found new employment. The admissions quota introduced in April 1933 for Jews at public schools and universities dramatically increased the need for Jewish education. Two thirds of all Jewish pupils were already attending a Jewish school in 1937, where they were prepared for a future outside of Germany. The support of emigration became one of the most important enterprises of the Reichsvertretung.

In October 1935, after Jews were excluded from the Winterhilfswerk des Deutschen Volkes (Winter Relief Organization of the German People), an effective organization, the Jüdische Winterhilfe (Jewish Winter Relief), arose: those in need were helped with heating material and clothing quickly and unbureaucratically; in the winter of 1936–1937, 30,000 people benefited from this assistance.

Jüdischer Kulturbund

In the summer of 1933, on the initiative of the theater director Kurt Baumann (1907–1983), the former substitute director of the Deutsche Oper, Kurt Singer (1885–1944) and the dramatic advisor and writer Julius Bab (1880–1955) together founded the Kulturbund deutscher Juden (Cultural Alliance of German Jews). Although the professional restrictions of the "Law to Reestablish Civil Servants" could not be immediately applied to the cultural sector, it did however lead to an increasing discrimination of Jewish writers, artists, and actors in their professional engagements. The National Socialist authorities had approved of the project under the condition that all costs for the cultural events program of "Jewish" actors for a "Jewish" public be self-financed; in 1935, an order from the Gestapo forced it to rename itself the Jüdischer Kulturbund (Jewish Cultural Alliance). The initiators

Game of Aliyah, with which children were prepared for emigration to Palestine, Berlin, 1930–34

right: Benefit for the Jewish Winter Relief in Berlin, 1937

were well aware of their project's ambiguity, yet the possibilities for activity and influence outweighed the doubts. "As far as I'm concerned," Julius Bab wrote to the writer Georg Hermann in May of 1933, "I'm trying to make the ghetto to which we've been undeniably and pretty much irrevocably confined a little bit more bearable for the moment."

When the Kulturbund opened its program on October 1, 1933 with a performance of Lessing's "Nathan the Wise," it already counted 12,500 members. Renowned representatives of German Jewry such as Leo Baeck, Martin Buber, Georg Hermann, Max Liebermann, Franz Oppenheimer, and Jakob Wasserman were honorary chairmen; members of every important Jewish organization were represented in the board. Berlin became a model: regional cultural alliances were soon founded everywhere in Germany, offering jobs to more than 2,000 artists—even if only on an occasional basis— and enabling its subscribers to experience a rich alternative cultural experience outside of the Nazi cultural establishment. Thus, the Kulturbund was able to socially and morally strengthen co-workers and public alike until it was compulsorily disbanded on September 11, 1941, only a few days before the German Jews were forced to wear the "yellow star."

Kurt Katsch as Nathan the Wise in the opening performance of the Cultural Alliance of German Jews in Berlin, October 1, 1933

Roll of fabric with the "Jewish star"

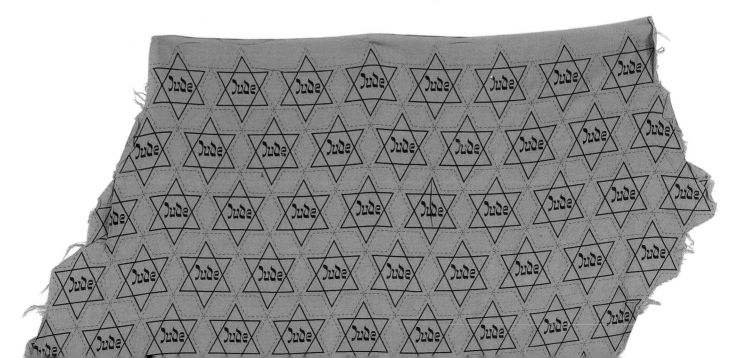

"Wear It With Pride, the Yellow Patch!"

The Kulturbund's activities found wide support in the Jewish media, which supported every measure to retain Jewish self-respect. Since the spring of 1933, the Jewish press had been calling more and more strongly for solidarity in an attempt to strengthen the sense of community: "Affirm Judaism," precisely now. And although around 1300 journalists lost their jobs in October 1933 when the German press establishment was forced to conform to the party line according to the "Schriftleitergesetz" (Editors' Law), the few Jewish newspapers remaining continued publishing and attempted to counter the defamation and agitation of the remainder of the press until they were ultimately forced to disband in November 1938.

The *Jüdische Rundschau* for example, which was founded in 1896 as the central organ of the German Zionists and appeared twice weekly, increased its edition from 10,000 copies in 1932 to 40,000 copies the year after. Its readers honored the courage with which this newspaper commented on the growing disenfranchisement. "Wear it with pride, the yellow patch!"—was the headline of Robert Weltsch's lead article, in which he called upon Jews to find a new sense of self: "Jews, pick up the Shield of David and wear it with honor." Weltsch demanded that a "Judaism under attack" remain true to itself. At the same time, however, the Jewish press acquired the role of providing information on emigration possibilities and demonstrating perspectives for the future—and thus giving hope.

Segregation was sealed with the Nuremberg "Racial Laws" of September 15, 1935. The "Law for the protection of German blood and German honor" prohibited, among other things, the marriage between Jews and non-Jews; "mixed" love relationships were punished as "Rassenschande" (racial disgrace). With its ideology of race, the "Law on Reich Citizenship" established the definition of the German citizen through heritage, degrading Jews to second-class citizens. The Nuremberg Laws led the Reichsvertretung to concentrate even more strongly on the demands for emigration, for it realized that a future in Germany no longer existed for the Jewish youth.

Within the Jewish community, the Zionist movement, which had been gathering experience in the practice of emigration for decades, won ground. Thus for example the Hechaluz (The Pioneer), a Zionist Palestine organization, had more than eighty Hachschara camps (Hebrew: training for a higher purpose) at its disposal, in which youths as well as adults were instructed in handicraft and agricultural professions in order to be equipped for the aliyah, the future in Palestine. Jewish youth organizations, the Jüdische Jugendhilfe (Jewish Youth Assistance), the Reichsvertretung, communities, and private supporters followed the example and founded numerous new training facilities.

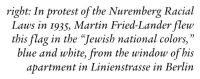

right: In protest of the Nuremberg Racial Laws in 1935, Martin Fried-Lander flew this flag in the "Jewish national colors," blue and white, from the window of his apartment in Linienstrasse in Berlin

far right: Possibly the remains of a decorative element of a Torah shield from the destroyed synagogue on the Fasanenstrasse, Berlin, found after the November Pogrom of 1938

Forced Into Emigration

"It was never a departure, but always a flight" was the observation made by the writer Adrienne Thomas, who had fled to France in 1933. Through its social and economic expulsion policies, the Nazi regime purposefully forced more and more Jews to emigrate.

Approximately 17,000 Jews of Polish nationality were arrested on October 27 and 28, 1938 by the Gestapo and deported out of Germany. Thousands of those expelled in the throes of this so-called Polish Action lived for months near Zbaszyn (Bentschen) on the German-Polish border. Those who had no relatives in Poland to take them in were lodged in horse stables and disused military barracks under catastrophic conditions; among them was the Grynszpan family from Hanover. Shaken by his family's fate, the 17 year-old Herschel Grynszpan attempted to assassinate Ernst von Rath, secretary of the German embassy in Paris. This assassination attempt provided the National Socialists with a welcome occasion for a state-organized pogrom against the German Jewish population. On November 9, 1938, 7500 stores and over 70 synagogues were destroyed all over Germany in a staged "outbreak of the people's rage." Another 200 synagogues went up in flames, 91 Jewish citizens were murdered, and several tens of thousands were arrested and carried off to concentration camps in Dachau, Buchenwald, or Sachsenhausen. In addition, the Jewish population had to come up with one billion Reichmarks as a "penalty," which was calculated as a percentage of the assets of each individual Jewish citizen; all insurance claims on the part of the injured parties were confiscated and store owners ordered to immediately remove all damage arising as a result of the "people's rage."

At the same time, the destruction of Jewish stores marked the end of the expulsion of Jews from the economy, which had been nearly completed by November 1938. From that point on, Jews were prohibited from carrying on any form of retail trade, mail-ordering, handicraft, market or fair business, as well as from visiting cultural events. The few Jewish firms that were still active were in the process of dissolution or "Aryanization." As a result, the German economy was practically "free of Jews."

While approximately 130,000 Jewish Germans had left the country up until and including 1938—most of them to the USA or Palestine, the only

Affidavit signed by Arthur C. Josephs for Heinz Rosenthal's emigration to the USA, New York, March 13, 1939. Rosenthal was murdered in Auschwitz in 1943.

country in which concrete preparations had been made to cope with a large wave of immigration—just as many fled following the November pogrom. The now unabashed expulsions provoked outrage abroad, as well, and some countries temporarily relaxed their immigration requirements. Thus, for example, in reaction to the November pogrom, the British government decided to admit an additional 10,000 children from Germany and Austria, whose transportation was organized by English aid societies in collaboration with the Reichvertretung—the majority of the children on the "Kindertransporte" never saw their parents again. The experiences of exile which left the deepest mark not only included the separation from relatives, the fear and insecurity over the fate of family and friends and the loss of the home country, but also the feeling of being unwelcome everywhere. As the pressure of immigration increased, the few host countries further tightened their conditions of admission, particularly financially; due to its unrestricted immigration policy, the international zone of Shanghai now became a vital place of refuge for a large number of German Jews. Around 15,000 refugees from Germany found an exile in far-away China, often plagued, however, by poverty, hunger, and disease.

For emigration organizations such as the Hilfsverein der deutschen Juden (Assistance Association of the German Jews) or the Reichsvertretung, which assisted the emigration process through

training, financial support, the procurement of papers, supplying the means of transportation, and working out escape routes, the emigration of such a large number of people was a masterpiece of organization. While more than a half a million observant Jews were living in Germany at the beginning of the "Third Reich," the census of 1939, which applied racial categories, registered 250,000 Jews. Most of those who remained did not wish to or could not emigrate—either they didn't want to leave their families behind, didn't have the financial means, or were too old to face the hardship of emigration.

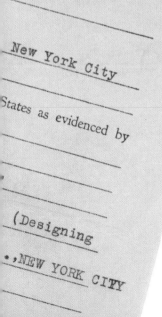

Obituary

I shall die, as most die;
The rake will pass through my
Life, and comb my name back into the soil.
Light, speechless, childless, I
Shall stare, weary-eyed, at the barren sky, ...

GERTRUD KOLMAR (1894–1943)
*was deported in 1943 and probably murdered in Auschwitz.
Her poetry, of which only a fraction was published during her lifetime, was in large part saved and published after 1945. "Obituary" was written between 1937 and 1940.*

New York City

States as evidenced by

(Designing

•, NEW YORK CITY

Mass Deportations

The persecution of Jews took on a new dimension with the approaching war. In the Berlin Reichstag on January 30, 1939, Hitler called for the "extermination of the Jewish race in Europe" in the case of war. With the "Law on Rental Conditions With Jews" from April 30, 1939, which laid down the immediate eviction of Jewish tenants in "Aryan" buildings, a new phase began in which ghettos were created and all Jews were concentrated in so-called Jew houses. The "concerted work deployment," which socially and racially defined groups were coerced into as early as 1938, regardless of their professional and physical qualifications, was expanded following the beginning of the war. From September 1940 on, all Jewish women and men were conscripted to forced labor mainly in the industrial and arms areas.

From September 19, 1941 onwards, one month before the first great wave of deportation, all Jews from the age of six were forced to wear a six-pointed yellow star the size of a palm, "visibly on the left breast of the article of clothing" and "securely sewn"; on October 23, 1941, all Jews still remaining in Germany and the occupied areas were prohibited from emigrating—both were preparatory measures for the mass deportations to the concentration and extermination camps, officially announced as "Umsiedlung" (repatriation) on October 24.

The Reichsvertretung, renamed Reichsvereinigung der Juden in Deutschland (National Association of Jews in Germany) in 1939, was forced by the German authorities to give bureaucratic assistance in registering, concentrating, and identifying Jews. In a desperate attempt to contain Gestapo violence, the organization cooperated. But by May 1942, when news of the mass extermination of the deported reached the Reichsvereinigung, it became clear that the strategy had failed. The leading members of the Reichsvereinigung were deported from January 1943 on, and on June 10, 1943, the organization was disbanded.

The first stationary gas chamber had already been built in mid-October 1941 in Belzec. Between December 1941 and September 1942, five more exter-

Sign advertising "Furnished Room for Rent" with the handwritten notice "Non-Aryan household," Berlin 1939–41

Suitcase belonging to Emma Levin of Berlin, which she took with her to Theresienstadt

mination camps were set up in the occupied areas of Eastern Europe—Kulmhof (Chelmo), Sobibor, Treblinka, Majdanek (Lublin), and Auschwitz-Birkenau, which was the largest. In the entire German Reich and in the occupied territories in Eastern and Western Europe, there was finally a total of 22 concentration camps with more than 1,200 outlying camps and commandos, in which the victims were exploited as slave laborers and tortured to death.

Resistance and Attempts at Survival

Numerous Jews defended themselves against the persecution and exterminatory measures of the Nazi state. They refused to take on the compulsory names of "Sara" and "Israel" or to wear the "star." Resistance extended from going into hiding and civil disobedience to active defense—and suicide. The so-called Fabrik-Aktion (factory action) in Berlin set the signal: in February 1943, all Jews still remaining and performing forced labor were arrested at their

right and above: The last letter from Martha Lieberman, the widow of Max Liebermann, to Erich Alenfeld, Berlin, March 4, 1943. Following her signature, it reads: "Picked up March 5, '43, in the morning! Took poison!"

underlay: Prisoner's jacket from Auschwitz belonging to Max Majer Sprecher

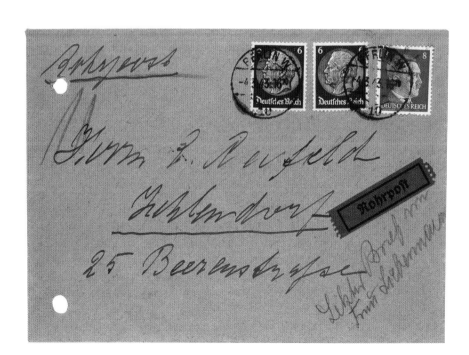

workplaces and deported to Auschwitz within a few days. Whoever could, tried to go into hiding. A legal existence for Jews in Germany was no longer possible, ecxept in the cases of so-called mixed marriages. It is estimated that only three out of ten in hiding survived illegality; most were denounced or discovered and subsequently deported. One of the groups that remained active up until the very end, organizing escapes or providing Jews in hiding with living quarters, documents, and food, was the Chug Chaluzi (Pioneer Circle). These Jewish youths surrounding the Zionist youth leader Yitzak Schwersenz (born 1915) had resisted deportation and were living illegally in the Berlin underground. Schwersenz, the leader of a youth alliance and a teacher, went underground in Berlin in the summer of 1942 with the approval of his national leadership. Forty young people followed him into hiding, man-

aging to get by until the war ended and constantly changing their lodgings; among other places, they hid in the domed roof of a tomb in the Jewish cemetery at Berlin Weissensee. Most of the group survived; Schwersenz himself managed to flee to Switzerland.

The Berlin resistance group around the young communist Herbert Baum (1912–1942) consisted of a circle of close political and personal friends. Since the autumn of 1941, members had been preparing for a life in illegality. At the same time, they demonstrated resistance with open political actions. The fire bombing of the anti-Soviet propaganda exhibition "The Soviet Paradise" in May 1942 set off a wave of arrests. Five hundred Berlin Jews were arrested by the Gestapo in retaliation; half of them were shot and the others deported. Between July 1942 and September 1943, twenty-two members

Briefcase with which Gerd Ehrlich fled across the "green border" to Switzerland in October 1943

of the group were executed, two had already died during interrogation—one of them Herbert Baum— and three were murdered in Auschwitz.

Genocide of European Jews

Apart from a few exceptions, the deportations consumed all Jews still remaining in Germany and the occupied territories. When the Allies began liberating the camps step by step beginning in mid-1944, millions of persons had been murdered by the National Socialists, among them six million European Jews. Only very shortly before liberation, when the camps in the East were cleared and the inmates transferred to camps inside the Reich in

anticipation of the approaching Red Army, many of those who had survived the torture up until then died along the death marches.

That Jewish life would ever again be possible in Germany following the mass extermination was inconceivable to the few survivors. Leo Baeck, the long-term chairman of the Reichsvertretung who survived Theresienstadt, formulated it thus in 1945: "It was our belief that the German and the Jewish spirit could meet on German ground and become a blessing through their marriage. This was an illusion—the epoch of Jews in Germany is over, once and for all."

Passport photographs of Jewish forced laborers in the firm Ehrich & Graetz, Berlin-Treptow, 1941–43

An employee saved the photographs of the former forced laborers in her firm. Following the war, she had carefully separated the pictures from the identification cards and preserved them in individual cellophane wrappers. In the late 1980s, she passed on the two boxes filled with the photographs to the Jewish Museum Berlin.

"And when they let him out of Sachsenhausen, I didn't recognize him. They gave him his papers with the order: 'You and your family have to get out of Germany within twenty-four hours'." Valid emigration papers, reports Rita Metis, who fled to Shanghai with her family as a child in 1938, offered the only possibility of release from the concentration camps.

Those who emigrated to Shanghai usually had no other choice. Following the November pogrom, the international zone of Shanghai became one of the most important sanctuaries for refugees. In contrast to the strict immigration policies of most other countries, if one was able to buy a ship's passage to China, or a ticket for the Trans-Siberian Railway, then all that was needed to reach Shanghai was a passport and a valid transit visa. By 1941, between 18,000 and 20,000 refugees had arrived in Shanghai, most of them from Germany and about a quarter from Austria.

right: Four Jewish doctors share a practice, Shanghai 1940

underlay: Detail from a map of Shanghai, ca. 1940

above: Placard listing the names of survivors of the Holocaust, 1946

Exile in Shanghai

Mr. Nobody, woodcut by David Ludwig Bloch, made during his exile in Shanghai in the 1940s

A Waiting-Room Existence

The refugees in Shanghai spent their lives in difficult conditions. Housed in ill-equipped barracks, many of them suffered from tropical diseases or under the extreme climate. The situation worsened when the Japanese military authorities set up a ghetto for Jewish refugees in the district of Honkew. But despite the adverse conditions, most emigrants were grateful to have found shelter in Shanghai, and tried to forget the distress and anguish of exile by organizing cultural activities.

Diverse forms of cultural life developed as different kinds of artists arrived in Shanghai between 1939 and 1947. Literary matinees, evening variety shows, and solo performances by singers, cabaret artists, and pianists were the most popular events. Theater plays and operas were performed in rented cinemas, dance halls, schools, and the refugees' living quarters. Stage sets and costumes had to be improvised. Suitable theater literature was also a rarity, so a variety of new texts were produced. About thirty plays were written, many of them comedies, offering the refugees at least a brief diversion from their plight.

End of Exile

When the Japanese occupation forces capitulated in August 1945, the Jewish refugees were finally able to move freely again. Now, however, the agonizing uncertainty about the fate of family members and friends turned into horror at the extent of German crimes and the knowledge that many of their relatives had been murdered.

After the end of the war, few refugees saw a future for themselves in Shanghai. Almost all of them hoped to travel on to America, Israel, or Australia, while a small number returned to Germany.

Tabernacle in the destroyed synagogue of Essen, 1948

"We are here"

Present Day Jewish Germany

Today I know that I had to happen upon this myself... that no one could have told me how it was ... This was the reason for the fear and the guilt of all the survivors. For it was human beings who had been able to do this, and we belonged to the same species." Along with the photographer Eric Schwab, the American writer Meyer Levin (1905-1981) took part as a war correspondent in the liberation of the concentration camps. Together they wanted to reach Theresienstadt as quickly as possible, where Schwab would find his mother. Yet on the way they came upon the death camps—Ohrdruf, Buchenwald, Dachau.

"Small as I was, I snuck past the box office window
of the only cinema in the camp, my heart beating wildly,
to see my first film: 'Mask in Blue,' with Marika Rökk."

SALOMON KORN
on his childhood in the DP Camp Zeilsheim

Following liberation, 1.5 million so-called
Displaced Persons (DPs), people who had been forcibly removed from their homes, came under Allied
care on German territory. The majority of them
soon returned to their home countries. Yet, for the
more than 50,000 Jewish survivors of mass extermination, the majority of whom came from Eastern
Europe, home no longer existed. Following 1945,
more than 150,000 Jews from Poland, Hungary,
Romania, or the Soviet Union continued collecting
in the reservoir Germany had now become.

Liberation reached only few survivors. When
the "Third Reich" surrendered May 8, 1945, no one
was prepared for the extent of the crimes. Only
gradually did Jewish historical commissions, such as
the one set up with the assistance of Joseph Wulf in
Poland in 1945, gather together the figures of the
murdered Jews of Europe. Out of an estimated six
million victims, some 200,000 came from Germany.

"Ibergang"

The British, French, and American Allies set up
temporary accommodation, the so-called Displaced
Persons' camps. The Jewish survivors, along with
many other deportees and forced laborers, sat here
on "packed suitcases"—an image that stuck for
decades with the Jews who remained in Germany.
Every place of residence was transitory. On the

*above: Photograph album of
David Minster from the DP Camp Ulm*

*left: Survivors celebrate Purim in the DP
camp Landsberg am Lech, 1946*

demand of concentration camp committees, Jewish DP camps were created in the US-occupied zone, such as those in Landsberg am Lech, Zeilsheim, and Feldafing. A new life emerged with hospitals, children's homes, synagogues, theaters, and schools. "Mir szeinen doh" was the slogan—we are here. Camp newspapers in Yiddish and Hebrew were established and named *Unterwegs* (On the Way) and *Ibergang* (Transition). Athletic clubs were also an expression of a new self-confidence. In the boxing tournament of the "Sherit Hapleitah" (the rest of the rescued) in the Circus Krone in Munich, Jewish survivors could test their own strength for the first time again.

Life in the camps remained makeshift. At a congress in Munich in 1946, Zalman Grinberg, representative of the Central Committee for Liberated Jews in the American zone, made the point: "We are still sitting in our camps as though in a vacuum... We have no state and no home. What the European crematoria didn't digest remains lodged in the throat of international politics." The resentment of the surrounding German society directly after the end of the war was also clearly palpable. On the occasion of a further congress of the liberated Jews in Bad Reichenhall in 1947, Josef Baumgartner, Minister for Agriculture in Bavaria, provoked laughs of approval at the "Tuesday Club," a forum for young politicians of the Christian Socialist Union (CSU): "We'll never be able to manage again without the Jews, and in particular without the Jewish businessmen in the USA and elsewhere in the world: we need them for the revival of our old business connections! As far as the Eastern Jews here in Bavaria go, there of course I'm of a different opinion: Gentlemen! I was unfortunately obliged to attend the Jewish congress in Reichenhall: the only pleasing element of the conference

Boxing gloves of Abe Malnik, with which he participated in the boxing championship "Sherit Hapleitah"

for me was the unanimously adopted resolution: 'Get out of Germany!'"

The camp committees organized emigration with the assistance of large Jewish organizations, for the most part Zionist. They negotiated with the allies to move the Jewish people out of the "slaughterhouse" as quickly as possible. The majority of survivors, however, were not able to meet the strict immigration requirements of the USA, for example, or of Great Britain and Palestine under the British mandate. In 1946, the Zionist leader David Ben Gurion traveled through the DP camps, urging the survivors to regard themselves from the "Jewish nation's standpoint": "You will play a decisive role in the struggle that lies ahead. You are ... a political power." The camps became the nuclei for a national consciousness that induced 200,000 people to embark upon the illegal immigration into Palestine. The dire situation in the German camps became a means of exerting pressure on international bodies such as the United Nations. Thus, the survivors, the deportees in the DP camps, contributed considerably to the founding of the state of Israel in 1948.

A New Beginning

Only a small number of German Jews had survived in the Reich itself, around 1500 of them in hiding and about 15,000 in marriages to non-Jews. Many of them had been baptized, had scarcely conceived of themselves as being Jewish, or had denied their Jewish identity. They were joined by around 9000 survivors from the concentration camps, who as German citizens were not admitted into the DP camps, and several hundred German Jewish returning emigrants, including those from the exile in Shanghai. Towards the end of the forties, these small, aged communities united with the remaining Jews from the DP camps, those who had not joined the exodus to Palestine or the USA. In the newly established communities, survivors from Eastern Europe soon formed the majority. In July of 1945, the

Israelite Cultural Community was founded in Munich, and a few months later, in December, a Jewish Community was established again in Berlin as well, one of whose founding fathers was the Auschwitz survivor Heinz Galinski (1912–1992). The express aim of these new establishments was their self-dissolution: in both the Western and the Soviet-occupied zones, the chief task of the communities was to aid in emigration and to ease the transitory existence.

Demonstration of solidarity with Israel in front of the Central Committee of Liberated Jews in Munich, 1948

Individual voices, however, such as that of Hans-Erich Fabian in 1947, began advocating a renewal of Jewish life in Germany: "There is no sense in constructing houses where huts are sufficient, and there is no purpose to building synagogues ... only to abandon them in the near future. The Jewish communities in Germany must make it clear that they are not just a transitory structure." For the majority of Jews world-wide, life in the country of the perpetrators was not acceptable, and the representatives of political Zionism regarded the development with skepticism. A clear signal, however, that some

Jews were beginning to unpack their suitcases was the founding of the Zentralrat der Juden in Deutschland (Central Council of Jews in Germany) in July 1950. As an official representative, this umbrella organization for the new Jewish communities and their local associations anchored the existence of a new Jewish community in the Federal Republic. Approximately 20,000 Jews lived in Germany, a number that increased to 30,000 community members in 1990.

"Reconciliation with the Jews,"
ticket to a rally in the Titania-Palast,
Berlin, February 17, 1952

Legal and Political Reappraisal

After the end of the war, a difficult and restrained confrontation with the immediate past began in Germany. In the Allied-occupied zones, later the Federal Republic of Germany (FRG) and the German Democratic Republic (GDR), various juridical, political, and cultural ways of dealing with what had happened developed.

Based on the Moscow Tripartite Declaration of October 1943 and the London Pact of 1945, the International Tribunal in Nuremberg was created. Following the trial of twenty-two Nazi figure heads, a large number of members of the professional class—doctors, lawyers, industrialists, and civil servants—were tried for war crimes in the subsequent twelve Nuremberg trials. These trials that probed the role of the "pillars of society" under National Socialism met with strong disapproval in the German public. 184 people were charged; 24 of them were sentenced to death, 12 were hanged, and 35 were acquitted—yet by 1956, all 98 prison sentences had been suspended. The public and political reaction to the Nuremberg trials fitted to the image of a West German post-war society that had found its way back to "normality" through the Cold War and the "Wirtschaftswunder" (economic miracle) with astonishing ease. "You can document yourself to death for the Germans, the most democratic of governments may be in power in Bonn—and the mass murderers walk around freely, have their little houses and grow flowers," the historian Joseph Wulf (1912–1974), who had emigrated from Poland to Berlin via Paris, wrote to his son in 1974, shortly before committing suicide.

In 1960, the trial of Adolf Eichmann in Israel drew public attention again: following a pointer from the chief public prosecutor of Hessen and Jewish emigrant Fritz Bauer (1903–1968), the Israeli secret service traced the SS member and head of the National Socialist department for "Jewish Matters" to Argentina and abducted him. Eichmann was sentenced to death before an Israeli court and was hanged in 1961. Since the end of the fifties, trials were once again taking place in Federal German courts, in which, however, individual guilt was judged according to German criminal law and not, as was the case in the Nuremberg trials, crimes against humanity. In the largest trial of the post-war era, the Auschwitz trial in Frankfurt initiated by Fritz Bauer, 385 witnesses, most of them Auschwitz survivors, were summoned to give evidence. The encounter with the perpetrators proved difficult for them, yet these trials marked an important step, as Gisela Böhm, one of the witnesses, wrote to the public prosecutors of Frankfurt in 1964: "It is sad as a survivor, an old former concentration camp number, to be worried about whether the truth is credible… Young people growing up now should know no hate, no mass hysteria—what happened in the extermination camps twenty years ago should never be repeated, never again."

A central theme of the political post-war debate was the question of reparations, the reimbursement and restitution of stolen property or wealth, and the compensation of losses. The newly founded GDR made no secret of the fact that a financial reparation would not be taken into consideration—born out of the spirit of anti-fascism, it did not consider itself to be responsible. Moreover, Jewish victims were considered to be passive "victims of fascism" and hence for the most part didn't share the special status of anti-fascists. Those "racially persecuted" by National Socialism did, however, receive increased pensions.

Already in the earliest days of the Federal Republic, questions of restitution were on the young democracy's agenda. For injustice incurred under National Socialism, the question of reparation was constitutionally regulated in the form of the restitution of seized property and compensation for "other damages." The Jewish Restitution Successor Organization, later the Claims Conference (CC), acted as trustees for the murdered Jews who had no heirs. On the one hand, new laws dealt with compensation claims lodged by individual men and women, and on the other with collective compensation. When the claim to reparation was anchored in 1952 following the Luxembourg Agreement between the FRG, Israel, and the Claims Conference, the Federal Republic paid a sum of 3 billion German marks over the following years to Israel, calculated according to the costs for the integration of survivors into Israeli society. The negotiations regarding compensation for forced laborers in the German industry and arms companies were only completed in 2001.

Anne Frank, Amsterdam, March 1941

underlay: Anne Frank Medallion,
Bat Mitzvah gift in the late 1950s

Culture of Memory

The most important thing for people both in the West and the East was reconstruction. Looking back was painful. And yet, in each of the post-war German states, the Nazi time was commemorated in different ways. The GDR regarded itself as the "other," better Germany, as having triumphed over fascism. The concentration camps were turned into national memorials of resistance, with the Jews playing only a peripheral role. In the Federal Republic, which viewed itself as part of the West and the legal successor to the Third Reich, "Versöhnung" (reconciliation) became the central key word. Discerning voices such as that of Lothar Kreißig, founder of the Aktion Sühnezeichen—Friedensdienste (Action Reconciliation Service for Peace), objected that "Versöhnung" hardly did justice to what had happened, and moreover could not be initiated by the former perpetrators.

In both countries, the respective ideological position emerged into the foreground, as is shown by the various models of commemoration: in the West, Anne Frank became a symbolic figure who resurrected once more a "belief in the good in people," in the salvation of humanity through the individual. A Jewish child became an icon of fascism in the GDR, as well. In Bruno Apitz' novel "Nackt unter Wölfen" (Naked Among Wolves), published in 1958, a three year-old Polish boy survives thanks to

communist prisoners in the concentration camp of
Buchenwald—his example was supposed to show
how the helpless individual can only be saved by the
collective.

In the cultural, literary, and public post-war
debate in the Federal Republic, intellectuals, writers,
and artists attempted to break through the silence
concerning the past and the suppression of
"German guilt." Writers such as Günter Grass and
Heinrich Böll, or the psychoanalysts and sociologists
Alexander and Margarete Mitscherlich confronted
pragmatic representatives of politics, business, the
church, and society who had elevated wealth and
"normality" to the highest axioms.

In the discussion about the ruptures in
German society, however, the few skeptical Jewish
voices such as Grete Weil, Edgar Hilsenrath, or Jean
Améry were scarcely heard. Some, such as the writer
Wolfgang Hildesheimer (1916–1991), member of the
Gruppe 47, left Germany. "I don't belong to the ma-
jority that is anti-Semitic, and I don't wish to be part
of the minority that accepts such a majority. In brief:
I don't want to belong," he wrote in 1963.

Instead, some of the returned Jewish emigrants, like Theodor W. Adorno, Hans Mayer, and
Ernst Bloch, became father figures for a young
German generation in the sixties rebelling against
the suppression of history their parents practised.

Bruno Apitz, "Naked among
Wolves," Rowohlt paperback,
Hamburg, 1961 and
"The Diary of Anne Frank,"
Fischer Bücherei, Frankfurt am
Main, 1958

"I wish to have no home on this earth;
perhaps my Jewishness manifests itself
nowhere more clearly than in this denial."

WOLFGANG HILDESHEIMER
Mein Judentum, 1978

"That was super." The popular television talkshow host Hans Rosenthal (1925–1987) in his show "Dalli-Dalli," 1985. Rosenthal survived the years 1943–45 in hiding in Berlin.

Following their return from exile in the USA, Max Horkheimer and the philosopher, sociologist, and composer Theodor W. Adorno (1903–1969) together founded anew the Institute for Sociological Research in Frankfurt am Main, famous as the "Frankfurt School." Adorno protested against an attitude that "creates an argument for anti-Semitism precisely through its public taboo concerning anti-Semitism." As long as a taboo exists, the danger of justifying it exists as well. This could only be countered by "not idealizing, not singing the praises of great Jewish figures or displaying pretty pictures of Israeli irrigation systems or *kibbutz* children."

For Germany, relations with Israel became a symbol for a new relationship with the Jews. The image of the strong, self-confident Israeli enjoyed growing popularity. When, however, Israeli troops occupied the Syrian Golan Heights, the West Bank, and Sinai in 1967, the political definitions of 'left' and 'right' floundered in confusion. While politics initially reacted in a pro-Israeli manner, there was broad support among the student protest movement for the Palestinian struggle against "Israeli-American imperialism." High-circulation newspapers rejoiced in the "Battle for Jerusalem"; the left was divided over solidarity with Israel or the Palestinians.

Coming Out

For the subsequent generations of Jews in Germany, their relationship to their parents' past and to Israel grew increasingly political, as well. The children of survivors felt growing up in Germany to be a burden; the magazine of the Zionist Youth spoke of Germany as a "cage." Their own parents had settled in the "land of the perpetrators," donated money to Israel, and were trying to inconspicuously blend in to German society. They didn't speak of their trauma, nor did anyone wish to hear about it. Many young people dreamed about doing it better themselves, of emigrating to Israel. Yet, with the Six Day War in 1967, this dream evaporated for many Jews, as well, and some returned sobered. The attitude towards

"In those days, I looked forward feverishly to the vacation camps (machanot) of the Zionist Youth of Germany (ZJD)... One thing has always remained: the comradery. Whenever I meet an old friend from the ZJD, it seems like yesterday."

GABRIELA FENYES
on her childhood in Hanover

Protest against the performance of Rainer Werner Fassbinder's play "Garbage, the City, and Death," photograph by Barbara Klemm, Frankfurt am Main, October 31, 1985

Israel remained one of solidarity, albeit with increasingly critical undertones.

The public debate that flared up around Rainer Werner Fassbinder's play "Der Müll, die Stadt, und der Tod" (Garbage, The City, and Death) in 1985 signified the first step out of the shadows for the Jewish community. One of the deliberately exaggerated main characters was a speculator called "the rich Jew," who was to lead the city of Frankfurt am Main to ruin. The Frankfurt battle over buildings in the seventies provided the backdrop, and many believed they recognized the real estate developer Ignatz Bubis in the depiction of the protagonist. In sentences like "am I, a Jew, supposed to wreak revenge on ordinary people?! So it shall be, and well and proper it is!!," an old anti-Semitic fantasy appeared in new clothes after the *Holocaust*, that of the Avenging Jew. Following Fassbinder's death in 1982, a Frankfurt theater wanted to perform the ambiguous play, which led to great controversy. On opening night, Jews of every generation took over the stage. This protest changed the self-image of Jews in Germany—with this step, they appeared publicly, more strongly than ever since the Holocaust, as politically-minded and active German citizens.

This new self-confidence was polarized in the nineties, among other things in the so-called Walser-Bubis debate. Ignatz Bubis (1927–1999), who survived the Holocaust in ghettos and forced labor camps, succeeded Heinz Galinski as chairman of the

Zentralrat der Juden in Deutschland in 1992. When, in 1998, the writer Martin Walser denounced the "moral battering ram of Auschwitz" and pleaded for "normality" during his acceptance speech for the Friedenspreis des Deutschen Buchhandels (the German Booksellers' Peace Prize) in the Frankfurt Paulskirche, Bubis and his wife were the only ones not to applaud him. Fierce debates followed, and for months the German newspapers were filled with the rekindled subject of "overcoming the past." The controversy was assuaged, yet for Bubis, who had fought for Jews to perceive themselves and be recognized as German citizens as a matter of course, the debate left deep traces.

"Of the five classes in our year, four were Catholic. All the minorities were combined in the fifth. While the Protestant kids had their religious instruction, four of us 'exotics' would play a kind of inter-faith soccer match."

MICHAEL BRENNER
on his childhood in Weiden

Since the fall of the Berlin Wall in 1989, German society has been in upheaval. The development has progressed from a traditional definition of "nation" and "citizenship" to a pluralistic civil society. The Jewish communities, as well, are no longer emigrant, but rather immigrant communities. Since 1990, more than 80,000 Jews have arrived in Germany with their families from the former Soviet Union. The "Russians" didn't come to Germany because history condemned them to do so, but rather because they want to make use of the chances an open Europe has to offer, just like any other immigrants.

As a representative of this new generation, the author Vladimir Kaminer (born 1967), who came to Berlin from Moscow in 1990, "recognized as a citizen of Jewish origin," documents this change. While the presence of Jews living in Germany today bears a symbolic weight, other minorities, ethnic or religious groups represent a far more significant demographic factor. In his book "Russendisko" (Russian Disco), published in 2000, Kaminer describes what unexpected effects media debates on "serious" problems such as the hostility to foreigners can have in society: "Suddenly a feeling of belonging together arises among a number of people who don't belong together, and never used to want to have anything to do with each other—Arabs, Jews, Chinese, Turks." One of the most important political and social changes began in 1999 with the reform of the German citizenship laws, almost ten years after the reunification of the two post-war German states.

The Jewish community today counts nearly 100,000 members, and with 10,000 members, Berlin once again is home to the largest community in Germany. Young Jews today tend not to ask the question "what is Jewish?," increasingly asking

*"Russian Disco" in the Kaffee Burger on Soviet
Army Day—Vladimir Kaminer plays hit songs,
photograph by Michael Kerstgens, Berlin, 2001*

"what is German?" instead. In the discussion about a
German "Leitkultur" or dominant culture—only one
of the public debates of recent years—Paul Spiegel,
Chairman of the Zentralrat der Juden in Deutschland, formulated the decisive counter-question:
"Is it really about culture, or a set of values shared by
the western democratic civilization which we have
enshrined in our constitution?"

German Jewish relations have been an important component of the symbolic politics of Germany
since World War II—of the questions about German
history and German society's sense of identity.
The Jews living in Germany today are both part of a
specific German history and tradition and a factor
in the transition towards an open, multi-ethnic, and
multi-cultural society.

"Memories of a Jewish childhood in
Germany? What occurs to me off-
hand is the Grüneburg Park. I know
that sounds very un-Jewish, very
German really; but that's how it was,
my childhood in Frankfurt."

NAOMI BUBIS
on her childhood in Frankfurt am Main

The Architectural Language of Daniel Libeskind

"Good architecture gives us breathing space, to speculate and to think of new ways of being."

DANIEL LIBESKIND

The new museum building, originally planned as an "extension of the Berlin Museum to house the Jewish Museum Department," began to incite interest among architecture enthusiasts and museum people even while it was still under construction. Thus, it seemed to follow as a matter of course that interest in the architecture of the Jewish Museum (which had since acquired independent status) would not just continue, but grow following completion of the most spectacular museum project of the 1990s in Berlin.

More than 350,000 visitors passed through the empty museum building, designed by Daniel Libeskind, while a team of historians, scholars, curators, and designers were still preparing the large opening exhibition: a windfall for architecture, architects, museum-goers, and the Jewish Museum. Where else is it possible to experience architecture directly, derobed of its functional context?

To many of the Museum's visitors, as they moved through its rooms, the articulation of space that colors, forms, and materials in the still empty exhibition floors yielded, provided an expansive frame of interpretation in which to understand and reflect individually on German Jewish history. As they formed their own interpretation of the architectural elements employed by Libeskind—the acute angles, unusual sightlines, spectacular window shapes, slanted walls and floors, narrowing and expanding rooms, the black slate, stripped concrete and graphite surfaces—many visitors thus began to fill the empty exhibition spaces in their imaginations. For the vast majority of visitors, the outer form of the building—its zig-zag structure, its titanium zinc facade slashed with the deeply inset and crisscrossing window hinges, which permit no recognition of the division of rooms or floors inside—expresses the intrinsic conception of the Jewish Museum. This is also true of the architectural elements that are visible from the outside: the Garden of Exile, the Paul Celan Courtyard, and the Holocaust Tower.

As early as the competition held to select the building's architects, Libeskind had worked out programmatically the manner in which these architectural elements would reflect the mission of the Jewish Museum. In his proposal, which he named "Between the Lines," he referred the building's "four-dimensional spiritual structure" to four sources of inspiration for its design. First, the architect saw a twisted star of David, like an invisible matrix, in the form that appears when one connects with a line the addresses of certain great figures of Berlin's cultural history, including Heinrich von Kleist, Heinrich Heine, Mies van der Rohe, Rahel Varnhagen, Friedrich Schleiermacher, and Paul Celan, on a map of the city of Berlin. Second, Libeskind sought with his design to complete Arnold Schoenberg's unfinished opera "Moses und Aaron." Third, he was thinking of the memorial book dedicated to the victims murdered in the Nazi concentration camps, kept in the

The Memory Void

federal archives in Koblenz. Finally, Walter Benjamin's "One-Way Street" influenced the building's design. The building itself is structured around "two lines of thinking, organization and relationship. One is a straight line, but broken into many fragments, the other is a tortuous line, but continuing indefinitely."

The Holocaust Tower
right: The Garden of Exile

At the intersection of these lines are empty spaces, or Voids, which form a significant organizational element of the Museum's floor plan. "The emptiness that I witnessed at the [Weissensee Jewish] cemetery," states Libeskind, "actually confirmed my idea of the 'void' as an architectural device. The 'voids' of the Museum provide a setting for nothing really to be displayed, because there is nothing really to be seen. It is just an emptiness which will never be eliminated from this city." The Voids rise vertically through all the floors and exhibition rooms. They thus invite visitors continually to contemplate the destruction of Jewish life in Germany by National Socialism, and to visualize this loss. With one exception, the Voids are inaccessible, formed of stripped concrete on the inside and coated with graphite. In the large, accessible Memory Void, which in its references to sacred architecture has reminded many visitors of Le Corbusier's chapel in Ronchamps, the Israeli artist Menashe Kadishman's (born 1932) steel sculpture "Shalekhet," Fallen Leaves, covers the entire floor.

The entrance to the Museum is through the baroque Kollegienhaus. The Libeskind building is hermetically sealed; one searches for an entrance in vain. Visitors are led through an inverted Void built into the Kollegienhaus, which is modeled in its rhombic form after the five Voids of the Libeskind building and which connects the old building with the new building. They descend a staircase deep into the basement, into a labyrinth of rising and tilting axes. The Axis of Continuity, which leads from the museum entrance to a wide terraced staircase and from there to the permanent exhibition space, forms a trunk from which the Axis of Exile and the Axis of the Holocaust branch off. Letters and personal articles testifying to the life of Jews before and during the "Third Reich," on display in glass show-cases set deep into the walls, create an emotional impact that intensifies at the end of the Axis of the Holocaust, as the visitor enters the Holocaust Tower—a bare, concrete tetrahedron rising the full height of the building. The sealed, unheated chamber is lit only by a narrow slit in one wall, high above the floor. City odors, traffic noise and the voices of children playing in the nearby park carry, subdued, into the empty space. Abandonment, doubt, fate, and helplessness all manifest themselves architecturally in the Holocaust Tower.

The Garden of Exile at the end of the rising Axis of Exile leads visitors into the open air; but the freedom so gained is pyrrhic and tarnished with a sense of extreme instability. The sloped grade and labyrinth of concrete stelae evoke the uprooting experience of exile. According to Libeskind, the Garden of Exile attempts "to completely disorient the visitor.

It represents a shipwreck of history. One enters it and finds the experience somewhat disturbing. Yes, it is unstable; one feels a little bit sick walking through it. But it is accurate, because that is what perfect order feels like when you leave the history of Berlin ... It is the only perfectly right-angled form in the entire building which has both right-angles in plan and right-angles in section, and yet it is the one form which I think people will feel strangely alienated from after experiencing it."

It was important to the architect that his metal, splintered building fit into the surrounding city space of south Friedrichstadt. The landscape architects Cornelia Müller and Jan Wehberg created a museum garden that surrounds the Museum with a variegated mixture of lawn and meadow, pavement and gravel, hedges and rosebushes, paths and vanishing lines made of railroad tracks. Around the Garden of Exile, where a dense cover of oleaster has cropped up on top of the pillars, a thicket of white and red roses blooms. The rose, a symbol of life, was

the only plant allowed to grow on the Temple
Mount in ancient Jerusalem. A playground for children, named after Walter Benjamin, was built in a
concavity of the building's south façade. Walking
along the east side of the Museum grounds, you
come across a Garden of Paradise, where a little
grove of locust trees has emerged naturally from the
scattered war debris. Finally, a courtyard that bears
the name of Paul Celan, a Jewish lyric poet, has been
incorporated into the passage between the Kollegienhaus and the Libeskind building. The courtyard
takes its shape from a ground relief of rough-hewn
stones, patterned after a graphic design by the
French artist Gisèle Celan-Lestrange. This ground
sculpture continues on the other side of the
building. A Paulownia (empress tree), Paul Celan's
favorite tree, has been planted on the border of the
rose thicket.

*right: The installation "Shalekhet"
by Menashe Kadishman, 1997–99*

Exile and Holocaust—The Exhibition in the Axes

The Axes in the basement of the Jewish Museum's Libeskind building symbolize architecturally the fate of German Jews in the 20th century: exile, Holocaust, and survival. The glass showcases set in the walls of the Axis of Exile and the Axis of the Holocaust form an intrinsic part of the architecture. They narrate the fates of a handful of German Jews, reminding us of the millions more who were driven into exile or murdered by the National Socialists. Nearly all the exhibits displayed in the Axes belong to the collection of the Jewish Museum and were donated by private individuals during the last few years. The correspondence between Jewish Museum staff and scores of donors bears witness to the emotional dimension that people frequently experience in parting with personal objects that evoke the memory of a deceased relation. When they donate such emotionally laden objects to an institution like the Jewish Museum, surviving relations are expressing their wish that a parent, cousin, or friend be remembered in the country where they had lived, and to which they felt they belonged. The biographical perspective of the exhibits in the Axes, which contrasts markedly with the thematic presentation of the permanent exhibition on the upper floors, attempts to fulfill this wish. The selected stories cannot be more than emblematic. In the future, the Museum will periodically change the objects and stories on display in the Axes.

*Photographs and documents
taken along by the Simon family
when they emigrated*

*right: The Axes
in the lower ground floor
of the Libeskind building*

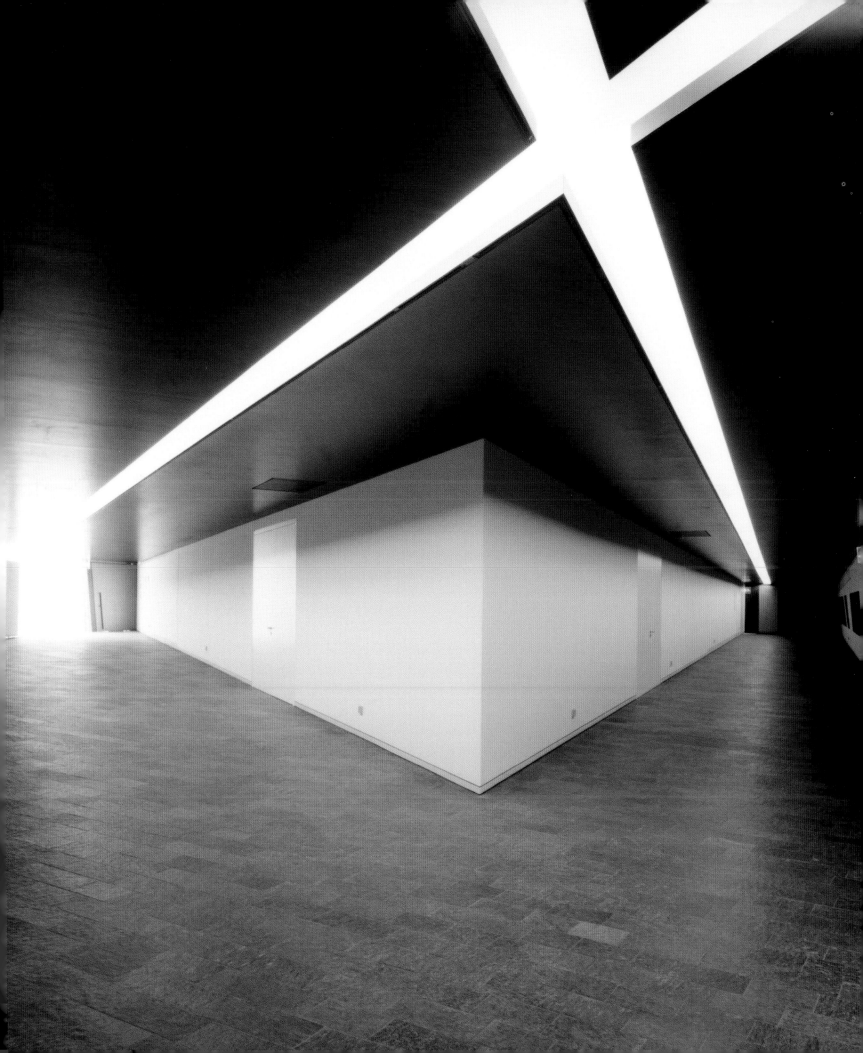

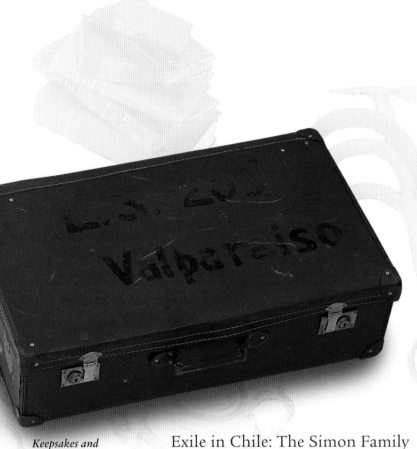

Keepsakes and practical goods taken along by the Simon family when they emigrated

Exile in Chile: The Simon Family

"A German Family of the Jewish Faith—Life in Germany, Emigration, and Return": this is how Herbert Simon titled the autobiographical records that he and his wife bequeathed, together with an extensive family memory chest, as a gift to the Jewish Museum Berlin in 1997. The Simon family's gift included documents, photographs, books, and various other family possessions. Ludwig and Martha Simon, their twelve-year-old son Herbert, and their relatives, the Kiewes, took these possessions with them from Berlin to Chile when they went into exile in 1939. The objects re-crossed the Atlantic in 1963, when the family returned to Germany.

In many respects, the story of the Simon family's emigration is typical of the fate of other German Jews who were driven into exile. Until the November Pogrom of 1938, the family felt no need to leave Germany; not until Ludwig Simon was arrested on November 11, 1938, and had spent one month in the concentration camp at Sachsenhausen before being released, did the family resolve to emigrate. Relatives of the Simons, who had moved to Chile immediately in 1933, obtained the necessary visas and papers, and provided support to the family when they arrived in South America. The Simons brought pieces of their old home and culture with them—not only books, including classics of German literature, household goods, and other effects of practical value to ease their life in an unknown country, but family photographs, keepsakes, and heirlooms of Ludwig's deceased grandparents from Bingen am Rhein. Following the death of her husband, Martha Simon returned to Germany, along with her son and daughter-in-law. Such a return was atypical, even exceptional. Most emigrants stayed in the countries that had given them asylum; many never again set foot in Germany after the war.

"Little Charlotte of Heilbronner Strasse":
Charlotte Ochs, née Friedlander
(1866–1943)

Charlotte Ochs was born into a well-established
Berlin family that owned a renowned retail silver
business, "Gebrüder Friedländer, Hofjuweliere Unter
den Linden." She married Siegfried Ochs (1858–1929),
the founder and director of the Berlin Philharmonic
Choir. They had four children together, who left
Germany one after another from 1933 onwards.
Charlotte Ochs visited her son Siegmund in London
in 1937, and shortly thereafter her son Werner in
Cape Town. After both visits, she returned to her
home in Heilbronner Strasse, where the family had
lived for many years. Between 1941 and 1943,
Charlotte Ochs wrote many letters to her daughter
Gertrud in Holland and to the mother of her
daughter-in-law in northern Germany. These letters
are unique documents. In them, Ochs describes her
daily life in Berlin, and also the daily incidents of
discrimination to which Jews were subjected and
which grew more and more invasive as time went on.
On January 28, 1943, she was deported to Theresienstadt. The last written sign of life we have from her is
a postcard, addressed to an acquaintance in Berlin,
which she apparently dropped from the train during
her deportation. The postcard reads: "My dears, I'm
badly hurt, a big suitcase fell on me today, deep
headwound, all wrapped up. So I've got a terrible
feverish chill, infernal pain. With love." Charlotte
Ochs died on March 2, 1943 in Theresienstadt as

a result of her head injury. Her daughter Gertrud
was deported from Holland to Theresienstadt
shortly thereafter. Later, Gertrud Ochs was moved
to Auschwitz and murdered. Charlotte Ochs' son
Siegmund collected his mother's last letters in an
album for the family following the war. Her grand-
son, Hans Reiche, donated the album to the Jewish
Museum Berlin in 1997.

*Title page of the album
"Our Mother's Last Letters,"
with a photograph of Charlotte Ochs,
1930s*

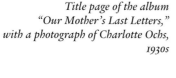

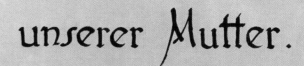

The Gallery of the Missing

Most cultures make a point of preserving objects and works that they believe mark the important understandings or achievements of their culture. Many of these items will migrate to museum collection building the cultural worth and reputation of these places. In the 19th and early 20th century bourgeois German Jewish people followed the tradition of the culture into which they believed, they were so thoroughly integrated by endowing German museums with their wealth and collections.

But all this changed in 1933. Over the next twelve years, the Jews of Europe and Germany were subjected to a violent campaign of exclusion, wanton destruction, and murder. As a result, much of the property of this culture, that might, in the traditional museum, be required to illustrate and support the history of these people, is exiled from the nation, destroyed, and fragmented. Therefore, the collections of the Jewish Museum Berlin are not rich in the normal sense of being comprehensive and containing a full set of representative objects.

But the process of the loss of these items is as much a part of the history of German Jews as are the achievements of these people. Indeed, it is a part of architect Daniel Libeskind's concept for the building, which is cut through by an empty space, the Void. The Void is Libeskind's way of recognizing symbolically that the destruction of the European Jews in the Holocaust has caused an absence, or void, in German and European society.

To capture and develop further this important idea, the Jewish Museum Berlin has formed a partnership with German contemporary artist Via Lewandowsky to initiate the idea of the Gallery of the Missing. In this Gallery, various stories of the loss of the sort of property that might form part of a museum's displays, and also the resilience of cultural values, are rendered as works of art available to all visitors. The works are displayed adjacent to the black walls of the Libeskind Voids.

Three installations initiate the Gallery of the Missing.

Via Lewandowsky (at left)
with a model of the glass cases
and the sculptor and engineer
Christian Schneider-Moll

left and below:
Model for the Gallery of the Missing

Encyclopaedia Judaica

Early in the year 1928, the first volume of the "Encyclopaedia Judaica" was issued. Fifteen volumes were planned in an enormous privately funded project that brought together editors and contributors from virtually the entire world of Jewish scholarship in Germany and Europe.

However, only the first ten volumes were published, covering the letter A to the entry "Lyra." In 1938, the project was brought to an abrupt end with the remaining 40,000 copies confiscated and destroyed by the National Socialist authorities. The 'Arch of German Jewry' remained incomplete.

After the war, not only Germany, but also the whole of Europe had lost its position as the center of Jewish knowledge. The scholarly network was destroyed with its members dispersed or murdered. Encyclopaedias published thereafter were edited in the United States or in Israel.

Head of the Sculpture "Hygiena" from the former Jewish Hospital, Frankfurt am Main

In 1914, the Israelitische Religionsgesellschaft (the orthodox Israelite Religious Society) built a new hospital in Frankfurt. With 200 beds and 7 medical departments it was one of the most advanced medical institutions in town. An exemplary institution, it attracted many gentile patients.

With the coming to power of the National Socialists in 1933, the function of medical service and welfare focused on the increasingly oppressed and excluded Jewish community. The forced sale of the hospital in 1939 saw it pass to the Frankfurt city administration. The Jewish community had to pay rent to continue using it. In 1942, the last Jewish patient and employee were deported. Towards the end of the war, the building was largely destroyed by bombing.

After the war, the ruins of the hospital were used to house survivors, mainly from the Ghetto Theresienstadt. The ruins were demolished in 1952 and a new building was constructed to house an old age home for the Frankfurt Jewish congregation. All that is left of the old hospital are two portions of columns, one showing the head of the Greek goddess Hygiena.

The National Socialists set out to destroy the Jewish tradition of welfare and support. However, while they wrought so much devastation, this cultural value lives on.

"The New Man"—Otto Freundlich

While of Jewish descent, Otto Freundlich (1878–1943) did not belong to the Jewish Community. Educated by his protestant step-mother, he broke with bourgeois society to join the circles of the avant-garde in Berlin, Munich, and Paris.

He created the plaster sculpture "The New Man" in 1912. By 1930, it was in the collection of the Hamburg Museum of Arts and Crafts.

On August 27, 1937, the work was taken from the museum as "degenerate art" and exhibited at the Nazi's "Degenerate Art" exhibition in Munich. Indeed, a photograph of the work, heavily shadowed to enhance 'racial' features, formed the cover of the exhibition catalogue. In this way, a work conceived as a message of the unity of human kind was coded in racist terms as "primitive," "Negro-art," "degenerate," "sick," "Jewish." In the wider artists' world it became an icon for the persecution of modern art by the Nazis.

After the exhibition, the sculpture disappeared. Otto Freundlich was murdered in Maidanek.

Via Lewandowsky

The artist Via Lewandowsky was born in Dresden in 1963 and studied at the Dresden University of Fine Arts from 1982 to 1987. From 1989 to 1995, he worked together with Pina Lewandowsky. He received stipends for the PS 1 Contemporary Art Center in New York City and the Banff Center for the Arts, Canada. Lewandowsky contributed to the exhibitions "Endlichkeit der Freiheit" (The Finiteness of Freedom, Berlin, 1991), "documenta IX" (Kassel, 1992), "Deutschlandbilder" (Images of Germany, Berlin, 1997), "Kunst des XX. Jahrhunderts: Ein Jahrhundert Kunst in Deutschland" (Art of the 20th Century: A Century of Art in Germany, Berlin, 1999). The artist also worked on exhibition projects in cooperation with scientific institutions, such as "Des Künstlers Hirn" (The Artist's Brain) at the Deutsches Museum Bonn (1998) or "Kosmos im Kopf: Gehirn und Denken" (Cosmos in the Head: The Brain and Thinking) at the Deutsches Hygienemuseum (Dresden, 2000).

opposite: Guide to the exhibition "Degenerate Art," Berlin, 1937, with Otto Freundlich's sculpture "The New Man" from 1912 on the title page

The Museum

The Collection

Silver Hevra Kaddisha cup, Hessia, 1914

"Jew in Prayer Shawl," painting by Lesser Ury, 1931

Although the Jewish Museum Berlin has existed as an independent institution only since 1999, its collection has a longer history: starting in the 1970s, the Berlin Museum and later the City Museum Foundation have been acquiring objects for their departments of Jewish history. These objects form the basis of the Jewish Museum's permanent collection today.

We are now working on expanding this collection. In order to convey a representative picture of Jewish history in Germany, we are collecting objects which above all tell stories, report on historical relationships, and preserve a sense of the cultural values, thoughts, and feelings of real people that we can recapture today. As a cultural historical collection, we place no limitations on the kind of objects that we may collect: ceremonial objects, graphic art, paintings, photographs, documents, everyday items, souvenirs, books, furniture, and handicrafts all find their place in our collection.

The collection extends to all regions and all epochs of German Jewish history. Nevertheless, the history of Jews in Germany and the history of our collection itself has led to concentration on certain areas. In the past, collecting activity centered on the Jewish history of Berlin. Owing to the significance of the city to this particular history as well as the location of the museum, Berlin history will remain a focus. However, from this basis, we shall extend the collection's scope to the entire field of German Jewish history in order to document regional diversity as well as the cross-regional relationships of German Jews. In this context, we shall also acquire selected objects pertaining to German Jewish history outside Germany, for example to Jewish life in exile, or in areas that belonged to Germany only temporarily, such as Posen and Silesia. Here, we look to

*Kiddush cup, with a
dedication to Rabbi
Elchanan Rosenstein,
partially gilded silver,
Berlin, 1863*

*Memor book,
Mirow in Mecklenburg,
1833/34–1897*

Shiviti plaque by Abraham Nisschand, 1925

*Office signs from the medical practice of
Dr. Oscar Hirschberg, 1895–1938*

document the German Jewry's connections with Jewish communities of other countries, as well as the role of the German language as a lingua franca for the Jewish community before 1914. Special attention is given to the 19th and 20th centuries, though the Jewish Museum has made it its mission to document the immediate past and present in its collections, as well.

Our collection also reflects the relationship between the history and culture of Jews, on the one hand, and non-Jews on the other. The borders are not easily discernible. At first glance, the work or life of an artist, or the business belonging to a Jewish entrepreneur, frequently presents a question: to what extent should this object or person be considered as

a part of Jewish history? Besides the representation of specifically Jewish life, however, the "non-Jewish Jews" as well as the themes of secularization and the cultural assimilation, even conversions, of a large part of the Jewish population, are historical phenomena that constitute a significant part of the history of Jews in Germany. The representation of such tensions belongs among the tasks of a Jewish museum in Germany.

The collection encompasses all facets of German Jewish history and culture, from everyday life to 'high' culture: science, art, and intellectual history. In addition to materials that testify to the public life of German Jews, in business, politics, science, art, and culture, the Jewish Museum collects

erg.
etc.

"Composition," painting by Otto Freundlich, 1938

"Young Israel of Dresden," painting by Carl Gottlieb Wäntig, 1820

underlay: "Couple," from the portfolio "In memory of Vilna, 1917," etching by Lasar Segall, 1917–22

objects and documents from the sphere of private life. The social conditions of the Jewish population in Germany induce us to focus on bourgeois culture. Another area of concentration, which suggests itself as a matter of course in a Jewish museum, lies in the collection of documents and artifacts of the Jewish religion and of Jewish institutions.

The collection has a threefold purpose: first, it maintains objects for display in the permanent and special exhibitions; second, it creates a representative overview of German Jewish history in its entirety; third, it serves as a resource for research. Our library provides a necessary foundation for all departments of the Jewish Museum. It is a specialized library, focusing on the history and culture of the Jews in Germany, accessible also to external scholars.

Over the course of the past decades, funding for the collection's growth has been provided by several sources: the Society for a Jewish Museum, the Berlin Senate, the Hauptstadtkulturfonds of the Federal Government and last, but not least, numerous private donors and lenders. The collection acquired a number of its highlights by virtue of support from the Foundation of the German Lottery in Berlin.

The largest and most diverse class of objects in the Museum's inventory was assembled almost exclusively from private donations. These objects—documents, keepsakes, household items, photographs, paintings, and much more—mirror the life and fate of Jewish families. Surviving relations have donated many personal items of this nature to the Museum. By so doing, they have helped make the

"Dutch Landscape," painting by Arthur Segal, 1926

left: Arthur Segal, "Self-Portrait with Brush and Palette," ca. 1941

Museum not just a place of collection and documentation, but a place of memory.

While the museum will continue to receive and rely on public support for its acquisitions, we have redoubled our efforts to solicit charitable contributions. Our contact with emigrants and private foundations has intensified over the past twelve months and led to several significant donations. In the future, we shall work harder to obtain funding for larger acquisitions by recruiting private sponsors to support individual projects. In this regard, we are particularly grateful to Dieter Rosenkranz, who made it possible for the Jewish Museum to present Menashe Kadishman's moving installation "Shalekhet."

Hans-Oskar Baron Löwenstein de Witt with the roll of fabric with the "Jewish star" that he gave to the museum, and Irene Lammel with the trunk that she used when she emigrated to England

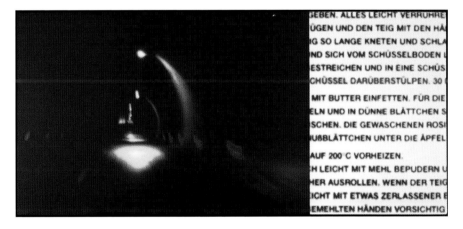

*"Time Station"
(dedicated to Milena Jesenská),
by Rivka Rinn,
mixed media on canvas, 1997*

The Archive of the Leo Baeck Institute in the Jewish Museum Berlin

With the establishment of a Berlin branch of the archive of the Leo Baeck Institute New York, the most important archive for German Jewish history will be made available in Germany. This will not only considerably extend the holdings of the Museum's own historical archive but also enrich Berlin and Germany with a collection of inestimable worth.

The Leo Baeck Institute was founded with branches in the three cities of New York, London, and Jerusalem in 1955 by the Council of Jews from Germany. Its aim was to advance research into the history of Jews in the German-speaking areas in Central Europe from the Enlightenment through the 20th century, to collect the necessary material, and to promote the publication of relevant studies. The Institute bears the name of the man who was the last leader of the Jewish community in Germany before the Second World War: Rabbi Leo Baeck (1873–1956). Toward the end of his life, he was president of the Council of Jews from Germany, Chairman of the World Union for Progressive Judaism, and the first president of the Institute named after him.

The archive of the Leo Baeck Institute contains the largest collection of material on the history of Jews in Germany, Austria and other German-speaking areas of Central Europe over the last 300 years. Approximately one million documents, including community records, personal papers, correspondence, and a wide variety of material on religious, social, cultural, intellectual, political, and economic subjects, cover the complete spectrum of German

"Leo Baeck," portrait
by Ludwig Meidner, 1931

*Writing desk, made by students
in the Jewish Training Workshop in
Frankfurt am Main, ca. 1937*

Jewry. In addition, the unique collection of over 1200 memoirs dating from 1790 to the present offers insight into all aspects of German Jewish daily life. The Institute also possesses a photo archive with more than 30,000 images, and a significant art collection with works by notable German Jewish artists, illustrators, and architects, and a large number of drawings by concentration camp prisoners.

Over the coming years, virtually all of the items in the archive will be accessible in the Jewish Museum Berlin, as reproductions and in part in their original form. This arrangement between the Leo Baeck Institute New York and the Jewish Museum Berlin is important because it will ease access for the increasing number of scholars and students from Germany and Europe who previously had to travel to New York in order to view the material. It must, however, also to be seen in the light of the tremendous growth in interest in German Jewish history over the past two decades among broad segments of German society. Furthermore, the return of documents and objects to their country of origin, more than sixty years after they were saved by emigrants who were forced into exile, is of great symbolic significance.

Both institutions will continue to collect additional material documenting German Jewish culture and history up to the present, to conduct research, to present their holdings to the public, and to preserve them for future generations.

The Departments
of the Museum

Education

*"Heaven's Fields,"
a play by and with
Adriana Altaras, in
the Jewish Museum
Berlin, May 2000*

History is a reconstruction of events by historians on the basis of available sources. In contrast to academic institutions, where textual sources furnish the primary data from which historians attempt to explain past events, historical museums rely primarily upon cultural artifacts that have more or less accidentally survived.

To a large extent, the set of tools used by a historian is defined by his methodology and by the

purposes and biases that motivate his research.
History can be used to provide advice in public
affairs, to justify economic, political, religious or
national interests, or to lay the foundation for
moralizing prophesies. In any event, history involves
both field research and detective work in archives or
collections. Insofar as history seeks out the
unknown, it can lead to discoveries that take a long
time to lay root in the public's consciousness. The
sociologist Emile Durkheim has described the
researcher's journey as follows: "The subject matter
of every science is discovery, and every discovery
disturbs, to a greater or lesser extent, commonly held
beliefs." With regard to a historical museum, this
means that exhibition visitors may, by virtue of the
objects presented, obtain unexpected and surprising
insights into times past that cause them to re-
evaluate assumptions they had taken for granted.
The Jewish Museum's education department has
developed a series of tours, workshops, films,
lectures, conferences, and colloquia with the inten-
tion of assisting and accompanying its visitors in
this adventure of discovery.

Research

The Jewish Museum Berlin plans to create a research
department in which scholars will study the history
of Jews in Germany and other topics related to the
mission of a Jewish museum. The Museum will
conduct research projects regarding its collection
and archives and in the preparation of exhibitions
and publications. Moreover, the research department
will periodically invite guest professors and make
available research grants to enable scholars from
Germany and abroad to study in the Museum. The
results of their research will be shared with the
Museum's staff and visitors in the form of publications, lectures, international symposia, workshops,
colloquia, and special exhibition projects.

The Rafael Roth Learning Center—
Interactive Learning
in the Jewish Museum Berlin

Rafael Roth,
engineer
and businessman

The Learning Center constitutes a virtual memory of the Jewish Museum: museum visitors can delve into an individualized world of historical data here. The information to be discovered expands continuously; each visit leads to an exciting encounter with German Judaism. The multimedia history presentations set out in search of footprints of Jewish life, providing insights into the workday, religion, and traditions of Jews. Together with achievements and successes of Jewish citizens, however, the Learning Center also presents the dark side of their tumultuous history in Germany: the perilous life of a minority throughout the centuries and the persecution and annihilation of Jewish life in the years 1933 to 1945. The Learning Center moreover concerns itself not exclusively with the past—it is also a place for questions and discussions about current affairs.

The Learning Center is located in the museum's lower ground floor, next to the Axes. It invites museum visitors of all ages to extend their experience of the permanent exhibition and learn more about Judaism, German Jewish culture and German Jewish history. Computer stations are available to investigate various themes. Those with special interests can also search the database for concepts, dates, or time periods.

There is even more: one can learn more about selected objects in the collection of the Jewish Museum Berlin through the Catalogue. Our visitors will find a warehouse of knowledge in the Fund. In articles, pictures, and other media, history is waiting to be discovered.

The concept of the Learning Center was developed by the Stuttgart firm Pandora Neue Medien GmbH. Its technical heart are a gigabit ethernet network and the central media data bank. Pandora created a content management system, *ORA*-Object Research Assistant, specifically for the Jewish Museum Berlin. This project was supported by Thunderwave Inc., Washington D.C. Computer stations are available for individuals, small groups, and classes. The computers are easy to use—but our hosts are also there to help you with any questions.

Please join us in the Learning Center for an exciting journey of discovery through German Jewish history and culture!

Temporary Exhibitions

In addition to the permanent exhibition, the Jewish Museum Berlin presents six to eight temporary exhibitions each year in the former Supreme Court of Justice building. In these exhibitions, the Museum can pursue more deeply and more broadly certain historical themes that the permanent exhibition may have only grazed or does not feature. It can also raise topics of significance to contemporary Jewish culture in Germany. The program thus encompasses exhibitions on German Jewish history, art and culture, photography or thematic art exhibitions, contemporary art and installations, historical exhibi-

tions on the Holocaust and exile. We accord special importance to our educational mission and are developing programs designed for children and young adults. Performances and multi-media presentations will accompany the exhibitions, to encourage repeated interaction with the Museum.

The Jewish Museum Berlin develops exhibitions in close cooperation with other Jewish museums in Germany as well as similar institutions throughout Europe, the United States, and Israel. It also exchanges objects and exhibits with these institutions, so that they are accessible to museumgoers in different places. The diversity of the Jewish Museum's programs, themes, performances, and media of expression will give a comprehensive insight into contemporary Jewish life in Germany and elsewhere.

right: "Surviving in Sarajevo. A Jewish Community Helps its City. Photographs by Edward Serotta," exhibited in the unfinished Libeskind building, April 30 through June 5, 1995

below: "Life in the Waiting Room. Exile in Shanghai, 1939–47." Exhibition in the Martin-Gropius Building in Berlin from July 4 through August 14, 1997

Museum Workshop for the Blind Otto Weidt

During the period of National Socialism, many Jewish and non-Jewish blind and deaf employees worked under the protection of the industrialist Otto Weidt, who produced brooms and brushes in a small factory—deemed "strategically important" by the war time regime—on Rosenthaler Strasse, number 39, near the Hackescher Markt in Berlin. His factory was often the last refuge for the workers and their families. At great risk to himself, Weidt fought to mitigate the plight of his workers: he rescued 'his' Jews from deportation compounds, hid a family of four in a back room of the factory, and helped one of his employees escape from a concentration camp.

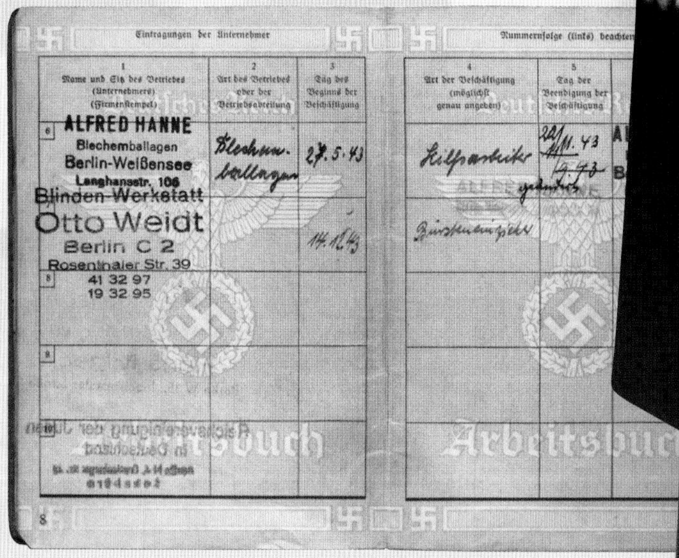
Eintragungen der Unternehmer
ALFRED HANNE
Blechemballagen
Berlin-Weißensee
Langhansstr. 105
Blinden-Werkstatt
Otto Weidt
Berlin C 2
Rosenthaler Str. 39
41 32 97
19 32 95
Arbeitsbuch

"Arbeitsbuch," the National Socialist employment book of Hans Israelowicz, until 1943

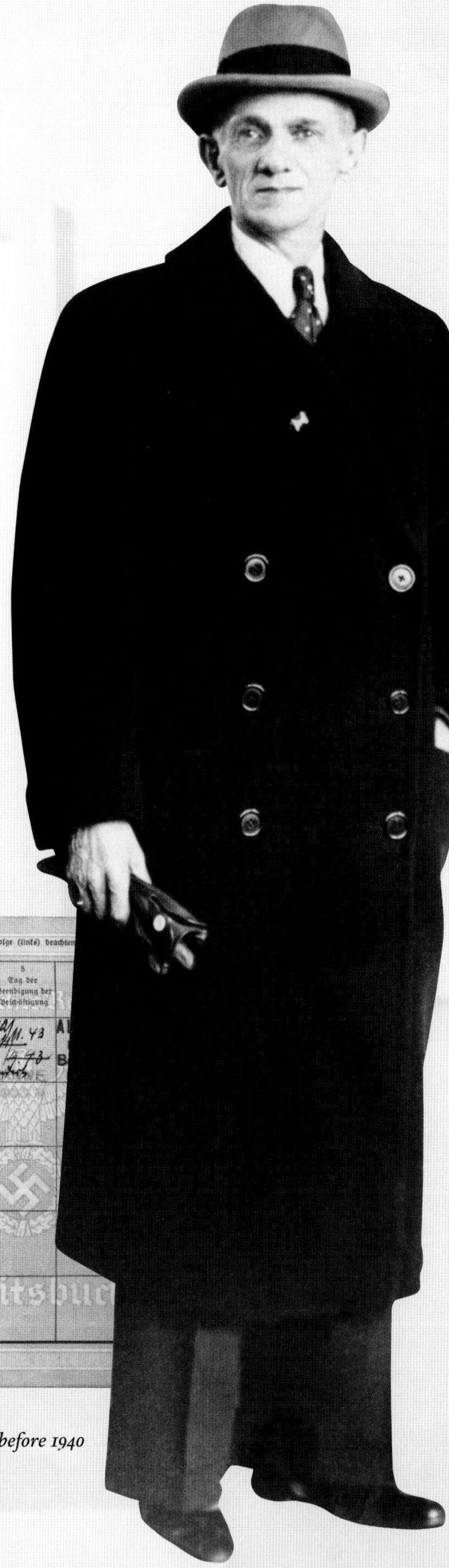

Otto Weidt, before 1940

Otto Weidt with his employees in the workshop, 1941.
First row, third from the right: Inge Deutschkron;
Second row, second and third from the right: Alice Licht and Otto Weidt;
Last row, first and second from the right: Max and Chaim Horn

Three rooms of Weidt's former factory have remained nearly untouched since the war. Students from the museology department of the Fachhochschule für Technik und Wirtschaft of Berlin (FHTW) helped to make these rooms accessible to the public. They created a place of remembrance, a memorial to the silent hero Otto Weidt and to the people he helped, on the authentic site of the factory.

Using letters, poems and photographs, an exhibition named "Blind Faith—Hidden at the Hackescher Markt 1941–1943" portrays the living conditions of people constantly threatened with deportation. The exhibition is based on the memoirs and testimony of eyewitnesses such as the German Israeli writer Inge Deutschkron, who worked as a secretary in Weidt's workshop for the blind from 1941 to 1943. In her book, Deutschkron relates stories about Weidt and his charges, including Alice Licht, Weidt's personal secretary and lover.

In 1943, Weidt rented a room on Neanderstrasse (today Heinrich-Heine-Strasse), ostensibly for use as a warehouse. Alice and her parents, Georg and Käthe Licht, lived in this warehouse for a time, hidden behind piles of brooms and brushes. Betrayed by an informer, Alice Licht and her parents were deported from Berlin to Theresienstadt on November 25, 1943, on the "98th Elderly Transport."

In January 1945, in the chaos that ensued when prisoners on one of the so-called death marches passed through the concentration camp in Christianstadt, Alice Licht managed to escape. She witnessed the liberation of Berlin together with Otto Weidt in his apartment in Zehlendorf.

Otto Weidt had already bribed officials of the Gestapo on many occasions prior to the commencement of deportations. When the Gestapo arrested all of the blind and deaf Jews working in his factory and held them in the nearby collection place on Grosse Hamburger Strasse, Weidt succeeded in freeing them with the payment of bribes.

The students of the FHTW met one important witness directly at the former factory site: Hans Israelowicz, who had worked in Weidt's workshop for the blind starting on December 19, 1943, had returned to his former workplace for the first time after 50 years.

Weidt also attempted to save the lives of the Horn family. Both father and son worked in the factory. When the family was ordered for deportation, Weidt hid them in the furthermost room of the factory, a storage room with no windows. A wardrobe masked the entrance to their hiding place: when one pushed the coats and clothing aside, the back of the cabinet could be removed. The Horns lived in this room from February to October 1943. Like the Lichts, the Horn family was betrayed by a Jewish informer. The family was deported on October 14, 1943, on the "44th Eastern Transport" from Berlin to Auschwitz. Presumably, they were all murdered there. Following the Horn incident, Otto Weidt was arrested.

Weidt championed the rights of Jewish citizens after the war as well. He built a Jewish orphanage and a home for elderly survivors of the concentration camps in Berlin-Niederschönhausen. Weidt, who died on December 22, 1947 at the age of 64, is honored as one of the "Righteous Among the Nations" in the Israeli memorial Yad Vashem. A long time went by, however, before Weidt's public service was recognized at the site of his actions in Berlin-Mitte. Finally, in 1993, a memorial dedicated to him was laid in front of the former site of his workshop at Rosenthaler Strasse 39, and his grave in Berlin-Zehlendorf was declared an honorary grave.

Originally undertaken as a student project, the Museum Workshop for the Blind Otto Weidt has been a branch of the Jewish Museum since January 1, 2001. As part of the Jewish Museum's education department, the Otto Weidt Museum focuses principally on groups of school children and young adults. Because so many blind and visually impaired

Museum Workshop for the Blind Otto Weidt in Berlin

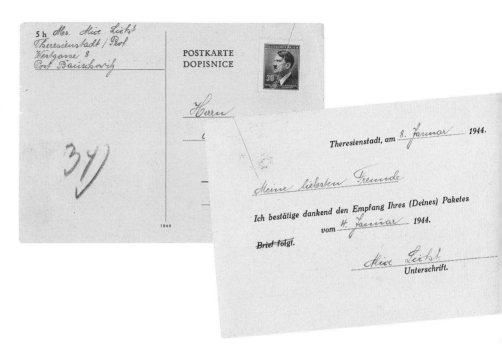

Postcard from Alice Licht to Otto Weidt, sent from Theresienstadt, January 8, 1944

people worked in the factory, the exhibition takes special account of the needs of these groups of visitors. A special program for blind and visually impaired visitors has been developed in cooperation with the Workshop for the Blind in Berlin-Steglitz. Furthermore, the Museum sponsors special events and offers guided tours of the former factory and historical sites in the vicinity of Rosenthaler Strasse. These events and tours are generally open to all visitors.

Address:
Museum Workshop for the Blind Otto Weidt
Rosenthaler Strasse 39
D-10170 Berlin
Telephone / Fax: (030) 28.59.94.07
E-mail: ausstellung@blindes-vertrauen.de
Website: www.blindes-vertrauen.de

Hours:
Tuesday–Friday from 1 pm to 4 pm
Saturday–Sunday from 1 pm to 7 pm
Tours upon request

Otto Weidt, Alice Licht and Gustav Kremmert in the office of the workshop, early 1940s

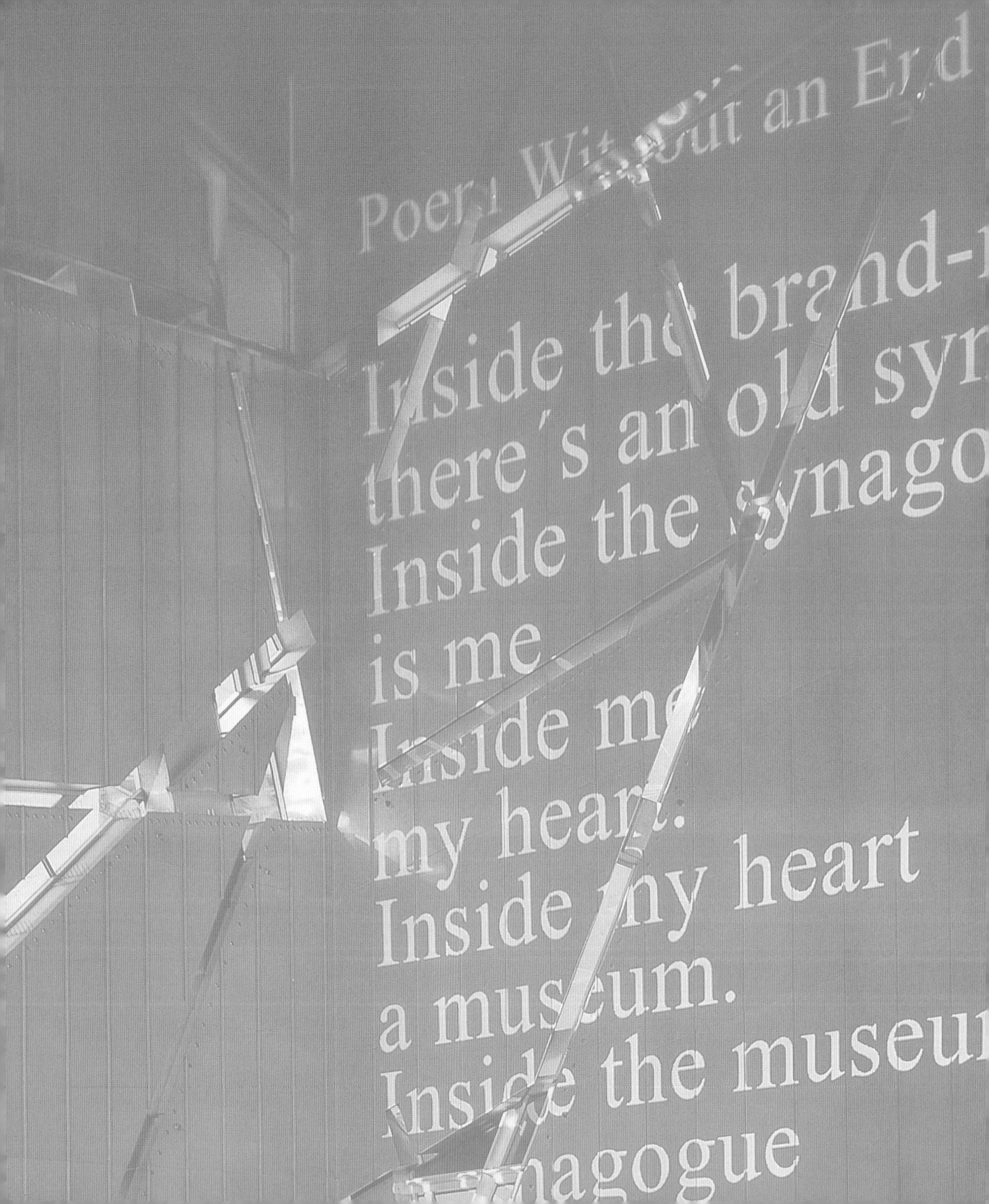

Poem Without an End

Inside the brand-n
there's an old syn
Inside the synago
is me.
Inside me
my heart.
Inside my heart
a museum.
Inside the museu
a synagogue

Aliyah Literally "ascent," refers to the settling of Palestine, later Israel

Ashkenazim The community of Jews descended from those living in Germany and France in the Middle Ages, and later in Eastern Europe

Bar Mitzvah/Bat Mitzvah Literally "son/daughter of the Covenant," a celebration by which a boy or girl is inducted into religious maturity

Besamin Box Spice box for the → Havdalah ceremony at the conclusion of → Shabbat

Barhes or Berhes → Hallah

Brit Milah Circumcision

Cantor The cantor or prayer-leader who leads a service in the → synagogue

Diaspora Greek for "dispersion," the Jewish community outside the land of Israel. The Hebrew word is galut

Displaced Person (DP) Person who was forcibly removed from his or her home by National Socialism or the consequences of World War II

Eretz Israel The Land of Israel

Ghetto Any neighborhood in which the members of a minority live as a result of social, legal or economic discrimination; originally, the Jewish Quarter in Venice

Halakhah Jewish religious law

Hallah Plaited bread, made from wheat flour and traditionally baked for → Shabbat, also called Barhes or Berhes in Southern Germany

Halutz A → Zionist pioneer who helps to resettle and rebuild Palestine

Hanukkah Candle-lighting festival in memory of the Maccabees' re-dedication of the Temple in Jerusalem

Hasidism Mystical-religious renewal movement, which arose in Eastern Europe during the 18th century

Haskalah The Jewish Enlightenment

Havdalah The end of → Shabbat

Heder Jewish elementary school

Hevra kaddisha Literally "holy union," the brotherhood or sisterhood in burial that a responsible friend or relative enters into in the event of illness or death

Holocaust The mass murder of European Jews. Literally "burnt offering" (ecclesiastical Latin from a Greek root); the Hebrew term is Shoah

Huppah Wedding canopy, under which the marriage ceremony takes place

Kabbalah Jewish mystical tradition, which was developed in Provence and Spain beginning in the 12th century c.e. and later also in Palestine

Kabbalat Shabbat Beginning of → Shabbat

Kaddish Prayer for the dead

Kashrut Regulations concerning ritual purity, especially the rules governing food consumption

Ketubbah Marriage contract, which defines the duties of a husband towards his wife in the event of divorce or death

Kibbutz Community settlement founded on a cooperative basis in Palestine, later Israel

Kiddush Literally "consecration," the blessing spoken over a glass of wine on → Shabbat and Jewish holidays

Kippah Covering for the head which is customary at prayer and in other religious activities

Kosher → Yiddish for "appropriate"; meaning in conformity with the rules of → Kashrut

Mappah Literally "cloth," → Torah binder, with which the Torah scroll is bound in the synagogue; also the name of the → Ashkenasi commentary, "tablecloth," to the → Shulhan Arukh, "the prepared table"

Maskilim Partisans or followers of the → Haskalah

Mazzah The unleavened bread eaten for → Pessah

Minyan The minimum quorum of ten adult men necessary to hold a religious service

Mishnah A corpus of exegeses of the → Torah that was developed and canonized in the Second century C. E.

Mitzvah Religious commandment

Mikveh Ritual bath

Parve Literally "neutral," a foodstuff that can be consumed with meat as well as with drairy according the → Kashrut

Pessah Celebration in memory of the Israelites' exodus from Egypt

Pogrom Russian for "destruction," any violent outlash against a population group

Purim Celebration in memory of the deliverance of the Persian Jews, recounted in the biblical Book of Ester

Rabbi Literally "my teacher," a Rabbi's duties include interpretation of the → Halakhah, religious instruction and spiritual guidance

Sephardim The community of Jews that are descended from those living in Spain and Portugal in the Middle Ages

Shabbat Day of celebration and rest, which begins on Friday at sundown and ends at sundown on Saturday

Shadhan Person who arranges marriages

Shtetl A small town Jewish community in Eastern Europe

Shulhan Arukh Literally "the prepared table," a summary of established Jewish religious law written by Joseph Caro in the 16th century

Sukkot Festival of the Tabernacle, celebrated in memory of the 40 years during which the Israelites wandered through the desert after the exodus from Egypt

Synagogue Greek for "gathering," this is the Jewish place of worship; the Hebrew term, Bet ha-Knesset, means "gathering house"

Talmud Interpretations and commentaries to the → Mishnah, written down in the 5th century C. E. in Babylonia and Palestine

Torah Literally "teaching," the five Books of Moses, and by extension the entire corpus of written biblical teachings

Torah Scribe Person who brings forth the → Torah scroll with the five Books of Moses, from which certain passages are read aloud during the Jewish religious service

Trefe Not → kosher

Yahrzeit Anniversary of a death, which is commemorated by a visit to the deceased's grave, the lighting of an anniversary candle and the incantation of the → Kaddish

Yeshivah → Talmud school

Yiddish Colloquial language of the → shtetl, deriving from middle high-German with Hebrew and Slavic elements

Zion Originally, the name of a hill in Jerusalem; later, a synonym for Jerusalem and the entire Holy Land

Zionism A nationalist movement that arose in the 19th century, with the goal of creating a Jewish state in Palestine

The Jewish Museum Berlin wishes to thank all of its donors and lenders. Donations and loans from the following private collectors and institutions are displayed in the Permanent Exhibition:

Donors

Irène Alenfeld
Antiquariat J. Reinhardt
Jutta Arend
Ellen and Erich Arndt
Gabriele Ascher Michels
Ralf Bachmann
Gad Beck
Fred Becker and Liesel Becker
    Sabloff
Regina Becker
Beiersdorf AG
Frans L. Benedick
Eva R. and Frederick E. Bergmann
Hermann and Mary Blaschko
Peter Bloch
Mona and Ruben Bollag
John Brahm
Hildegard Brilling
Henryk M. Broder
Edith ten Bruggencate
Burchardt'sche Erbengemeinschaft
Toni Vera Cordier

Gisela Dahms
Marlies Danziger, née Kallmann
Jürgen Dittmar
Dresdner Bank AG
Margarete Drewes
Johanna Eggert
Vivian Ert Bolten Herz
Sabine Fechter
Susan U. Fischel,
    née Ursula Neumann
Angelika Fischer
Dorothee Fliess
Thomas Föhl
Vincent C. Frank-Steiner
Frankfurt Marriott Hotel
Falk Gadiesh, formerly Grünfeld
Rosalie Gehrike
Wolfgang H. Geisse
Katja Gerson
Eva Gluckman, née Luft
Miriam Goldmann
Annerien Groenendijk
Ruth Gumpel

Eva and Frithjof Haas
Gerda Haas
Renate Haas and Hans Höfler
Mary Harber
Cordula Herbst-Stenger
Monica Herrnfeld Oppenheim
Ernest G. Heppner
Hanns-Peter Herz
Charlotte Herzfeld
Christoph Hinckeldey
Werner Hirsch
Historisches Institut der
    Deutschen Bank
Alex Hochhäuser
Rabbiner Hochwald
Guy and Irene Hofstein
Hotel Intercontinental Berlin
Otti E. Jarislowsky, née Arons
Seev Jacob
Manfred Jahn
Jeanette-Wolff-Heim, Berlin
Frieda Kaeber
Max Kallmann
Susanne Kester, née Luft
Hillel Kempler
Ayya Khema
Harry Kindermann
Anneli Kirsen
Walter Klünner
Ilse Laatz-Krumnow
Ernest R. Kunney
Shlomo Kurliandschik
Paul Kuttner

Marga Lakritz, née Gussinoff
Inge Lammel
Landeszentralbank in Berlin
Lotte Laserstein
Rudi Leavor, formerly Librowicz
Wolfgang Lehmann
Leiser Handelsgesellschaft mbH
Ernst Lenart
Renate Lenart
Leo-Baeck-Traditionsloge
Abraham Hans Levy
Walter Levy
Daniel Libeskind
Elfriede Lilie
Lions-Club Alexanderplatz
Georg Lippmann
Hans-Oskar Baron Löwenstein-
    de Witt
Tony G. Marcy
Shimshon S(igismund) Marcus
Ursula Marshall-Hoffmann
Alexander Maerzon
Hilda Mattei, née Meschelsohn
Hans Peter Messerschmidt
Erica Minster-Peyou
George L. Mosse
Museum für Glaskunst, Lauscha
Sonja Mühlberger
Manfred Naftalie
June Neuberger
Günter Nobel
Henry A. Oertelt
Rita Opitz
John F. and Hertha Oppenheimer
OSRAM GmbH

Hedwig Pachter
Hilde Pearton
Steffi Pinkus and Evelyne Pinkus
    in memory of Heinrich and
    Else Lewin, née Lesser, who
    perished in the holocaust
Peter H. Plesch
Rosl Porzky
Projektarchiv Oldenburg
Erna Proskauer
Harry Purath
Dr. Thomas Rahe
Rakusen's Kosher Food Company
Hans Reiche
Barbara Rosenbaum
Kurt Rosenbaum
Mirjam Rosenberg, née Beck
Dieter and Si Rosenkranz
Otto Ross
Ilan Roth
Rosa M. Sacharin
Gunther Schenkel
Heinz Schleich
Ursula Schlochauer-Nelson
Werner Schmidt
Brigitte Schmitt
Jizchak Schwersenz

Aviva Segal
Klaus Siepert
Lothar Sieskind
Felix Simmenauer
Carla and Stefan Helmut Simon
    in memory of their parents,
    Walter and Helene Simon,
    who perished in the holocaust
Herbert and Elisabeth Simon
Ilona Simon Strimber
Société Coopérative Vigneronne
    des Grandes Caves, Richon-le-
    Zion & Zichron-Jacob Ltd.
Society for a Jewish Museum
    Berlin
Erhard Stern
Stiftung Deutsche Klassenlotterie
    Berlin
Südzucker AG
Burkhard Sülzen
Marie Louise Surek-Becker
Heinz Ralf Unger,
    grandson of Leopold Brinnitzer
Renate Ursell, née Zander
Gretel Verhoek
Gerry Waldston,
    formerly Waldstein
Werner Weigl
Siegbert Weinberger
Die Welt
Agnes Wergin
Roselotte Winterfeldt,
    née Lehmann
Elfriede Wolff
Fritz A. Wolff
Raymond Wolff
Lili Wronker
Brenda Zobris

Lenders

Germany
Allgemeine Jüdische Wochen-
  zeitung, Berlin
Archäologisches Landesmuseum
  Mecklenburg-Vorpommern,
  Lübstorf
Archiv zur Geschichte der
  Max-Planck-Gesellschaft, Berlin
Klaus and Renée Arons
Bankhaus Sal. Oppenheim jr. Cie.,
  Köln
Bayerische Staatsbibliothek
  München
Berlinische Galerie, Landes-
  museum für Moderne Kunst,
  Architektur und Photographie
Andrzej Bodek
Naomi Bodemann-Ostow
Ursula Böhme
Michael Brenner
Micha Brumlik
Deutsches Historisches Museum,
  Berlin
Deutsches Museum, München
Deutsches Technikmuseum Berlin
Felix Escher
Gabriela Fenyes
Filmmuseum Potsdam
Freie Universität Berlin, Präsidium
Thomas Friedrich
Fürst zu Salm-Salm

Henry Gawlik
Gedenkstätte Buchenwald,
  Weimar-Buchenwald
Georg-Kolbe-Museum, Berlin
Joachim Haberland
Hamburger Kunsthalle
Familie Hartwig
Manuel Herz
Historisches Archiv der
  Hapag-Lloyd AG, Hamburg
Historisches Museum der Pfalz,
  Speyer
Historisches Museum Dinkels-
  bühl
Alex Hochhäuser
Susanne Horst
Jewish Claims Conference
  Nachfolgeorganisation, Berlin
Jüdische Gemeinde zu Berlin
Jüdisches Museum Rendsburg
Jugendbegegnungsstätte Anne
  Frank, Frankfurt am Main
Margarete Kaczmarczyck
Gisela and Dieter E. Kesper
Kestner-Museum Hannover
Hans-Dieter Kirchholtes
Elisa Klapheck
Kloster Stift zum Heiligengrabe,
  Stiftskirche, Heiligengrabe
Helmut Köhler
Kölnisches Stadtmuseum
Cilly Kugelmann

Simone Ladwig-Winters
Landesarchiv Berlin
Landesarchiv Schleswig-Holstein,
  Schleswig
Landeshauptarchiv Schwerin
Landesmuseum Mainz
Leiser Handelsgesellschaft mbH
Literatur- and Kunstinstitut
  Hombroich
Hanno Loewy
Peter Loewy
Magnus-Hirschfeld-Gesellschaft
  e.V., Forschungsstelle zur
  Geschichte der Sexualwissen-
  schaft, Berlin
Mendelssohn-Gesellschaft Berlin
Militärhistorisches Museum der
  Bundeswehr in Dresden
Montfort-Museum Tettnang
Museum für Angewandte Kunst,
  Frankfurt am Main
Museum für Hamburgische
  Geschichte
Museum für Kunst und Kultur-
  geschichte der Stadt Dortmund
Museum für Naturkunde der
  Humboldt-Universität zu Berlin
  · Institut für Mineralogie
  · Institut für Systematische
    Zoologie
Museum im Gotischen Haus,
  Bad Homburg v.d. Höhe
Museumsdorf Cloppenburg—
  Niedersächsisches Freilicht-
  museum

Prof. Dr. Kurt Nemitz
Neues Stadtmuseum,
    Landsberg am Lech
Oderlandmuseum Bad Freienwalde
Peter Oelsner
Horst Olbrich
Heiner Otterbach
Paul-Ehrlich-Institut, Langen
Philharmonischer Chor Berlin
Bernd Philipsen
Babette Quinkert
Andreas Reinke
Reiss-Museum Mannheim
Gert Rosenthal
Naomi Tereza Salmon
Sammlung Deutsche Bank
Sammlung Raymond Wolff
Jakob Schenavsky
Schleswig-Holsteinische Landes-
    museen Schloss Gottorf,
    Schleswig
Florian Schmaltz
Daniel Schnapp
David Schnapp
Richard Chaim Schneider

Bernd Schulz
Senatskanzlei Berlin
SPD Landesverband Berlin/
    Kreis Kreuzberg
Spielzeugmuseum Nürnberg
Staatliche Museen zu Berlin—
    Preußischer Kulturbesitz
    · Münzkabinett
    · Museum Europäischer Kulturen
    · Museum für Vor- und Früh-
    geschichte
Staatsanwaltschaft beim Land-
    gericht Frankfurt am Main
Staatsbibliothek zu Berlin—
    Preußischer Kulturbesitz
    · Musikabteilung
    mit Mendelssohn-Archiv
    · Orientabteilung
Stadt Ichenhausen
Stadt Leimen
Stadtarchiv Ludwigsburg
Stadtmuseum Düsseldorf
Marie-Louise Steinschneider
Stiftung Archiv der Akademie
    der Künste Berlin
    · Archivabteilung Darstellende
    Kunst
    · Historisches und
    Verwaltungs-
    archiv
    · Kunstsammlung

Stiftung Ehemalige Synagoge
    Ichenhausen
Stiftung "Neue Synagoge Berlin—
    Centrum Judaicum"
Stiftung Stadtmuseum Berlin
Theaterwissenschaftliche Samm-
    lung/Universität zu Köln
Todesmarschmuseum Belower
    Wald, Stiftung Brandenburgi-
    sche Gedenkstätten, Wittstock
Cord Christian Troebst
Volksbund Deutsche Kriegs-
    gräberfürsorge e.V., Kassel
Volkstheater Rostock
Moishe Waks
Susanne Willems
Württembergische Landes-
    bibliothek, Stuttgart
Württembergisches Landes-
    museum, Stuttgart
Christine Zahn
Zentralarchiv zur Erforschung der
    Geschichte der Juden in
    Deutschland, Heidelberg

France
Musée Alsacien, Strasbourg
Société d'Histoire des Israélites
    d'Alsace et de Lorraine,
    Strasbourg

Great Britain
Judie Cole
Sir Alexander Goehr
MEMORIAL SCROLLS TRUST/
    Westminster Synagogue,
    London
Richard B. Tait

Israel
Mary-Clare Adam Murvitz
Chava Amit
The Central Archives for the
    History of the Jewish People,
    Jerusalem
Yitzhak Einhorn
Dr. Uriel P. Federbush
Gross Family Collection
The Israel Goor Theatre Archives
    and Museum, Jerusalem
The Israel Museum, Jerusalem
Gabriel Levin
Rachel & Jonathan Moller
Michael Oppenheimer
Salomon Pappenheim
Mirjam Rosenberg
Ilan Roth Collection
Torben Samson
The Society for the Commemo-
    ration of Max I. Bodenheimer
    and Hannah Henriette Boden-
    heimer in Jerusalem

Canada
Beth Tzedec Reuben & Helene
Dennis Museum/ Cecil Roth
    Collection, Toronto

The Netherlands
Prof. Dr. W. D. H. Asser
Collection of the Jewish Historical
Museum, Amsterdam

Austria
Arnold Schönberg Center, Wien
Österreichisches Theatermuseum,
    Wien

Poland
The Auschwitz-Birkenau State
    Museum, Oświęcim

Switzerland
Cordula Maria Herbst-Stenger
Stephen Herz
Philosophisches Seminar der
    Universität Zürich, Hermann
    Cohen-Archiv
Schweizerisches Israelitisches
    Alters- und Pflegeheim
    Lengnau

USA
Sibylle Ehrlich
Friends of the Jewish Museum
    Berlin, Princeton
Leonard and Brigitte Freed
Prof. Dr. John H. Herz
Alice Hirschler
Sadie Hofstein, née Rurka
Otti E. Jarislowsky, née Arons
Stephen A. Jarislowsky
The Jewish Museum New York
Judaica Collection of
    Chaim and Naomi Steinberger
Leo Baeck Institute, New York
Mikael Levin
Abe Malnik
Alina Rocha Menocal and
    Christopher Rossbach
Ernest Michael
Hans Eugen Panofsky
Arthur A. Schwartz

Vatican
Biblioteca Apostolica Vaticana

*We would also like to thank those
donors and lenders who wish to
remain anonymous.*

List as of July 2001

We would like to express our gratitude to the following people for their contribution to and support of this book

The researchers of the Permanent Exhibition
Bernd Braun, Simone Erpel, Dr. Felix Escher, Dr. Jörg H. Fehrs, Thomas Friedrich (head of research), Miriam Goldmann, Karin Grimme, Sarah Hiron, Dr. Uri Kaufmann, Maren Krüger, Sibylle Kußmaul, Dr. Hanno Loewy, Léontine Meijer, Horst Olbrich, Dr. Sylvia Rogge-Gau, Barbara Rösch, Dr. Jutta Strauss, Jan-Christian Schwarz, Raymond Wolff, and Christine Zahn

The staff of the Jewish Museum Berlin
Claudia Assmann, Dr. Vera Bendt, Inka Bertz, Christiane Birkert, Naomi Bodemann-Ostow, Dr. Iris Blochel, Helmuth F. Braun, Lothar Brokof, Nurcan Bulut, Georg Burgstaller, Nigel Cox, Barbara Decker, Joshua Derman, Dr. Arno Dettmers, Dr. Martina Dillmann, Gelia Eisert, Gisela Freydank, Michal S. Friedlander, Regina Gelbert, Hartmut Götze, Ken Gorbey, Kai Gruzdz, Edda Herzog, Michael Hinz, Veronique Hinzberg, Sabine Hollburg, Annette Jobst, Barbara Kersting, Stephanie Kluth, Katharina Koch, Kathleen Köhler, Henriette Kolb, Waltraud Kratzenberg, Cilly Kugelmann, Sabine Kühl, Ariane Kwasigroch, Gisela Lemke, Theresia Lutz, Eveline Mahler, Leonore Maier, Gisela Märtz, Marion Meyer, Aubrey Pomerance, Timo Reinfrank, Hanne Reinhardt, Miriam Rossius, Margarete Sabeck, Karin Sakowski-Middelhoek, Peter Sauerbaum, Bettina Schob, Christina Scholten, Petra Schramm, Eva Söderman, Ulrike Sonnemann, Antje Spielhagen, Dr. Gerhard Stahr, Marie-Luise Surek-Becker, Jürgen Thuns, Dr. Sabine Vogel, Ernst Wittmann, Kathrin Zinkmann, as well as all other staff of the Jewish Museum Berlin

And furthermore
Prof. Dr. Michael Brenner, Ingke Brodersen, Dr. Rüdiger Dammann, Rainer Groothuis, Sabine Haack, Jutta Harms, Andrea Köhrsen, Hanna Kronberg, Gabriele Kronenberg, Andreas Krüger, Petra Kruse, Birgit Lütticke, Maja Majer-Wallat, Rebecca Morrison, Dr. Michael Naumann, Ulli Neutzling, Antje Pratesi, Prof. Dr. Monika Richarz, Prof. Dr. Reinhard Rürup, Petra Rösgen, Ernestine von Salomon, Andrea Scrima, Ralf Schnarrenberger, Dr. Tilman Spengler, Heinz-Josef Stork, Darrell Wilkins, Petra Winderoll, and Jens Ziehe

The Jewish Museum Berlin extends its thanks to all institutions and individuals who have contributed to, advised in, and supported the preparations for the Permanent Exhibition. Special thanks are owed to the donors and lenders, as well as the academic advisory board.

Academic Advisory Board of the Stiftung Jüdisches Museum Berlin
Prof. Dr. Wolfgang Benz, Berlin
Prof. Dr. Michael Brenner, München
Prof. Dr. Dan Diner, Leipzig and Beer Sheva
Prof. Dr. Saul Friedländer, Tel Aviv and Los Angeles
Prof. Dr. Michael A. Meyer, Cincinnati
Prof. Dr. Monika Richarz, Hamburg
Prof. Dr. Reinhard Rürup, Berlin
Prof. Dr. Peter Schäfer, Berlin and Princeton
Prof. Dr. Fritz Stern, New York

A scholarly catalogue is in preparation

Third Edition 2005
© 2001 by
Stiftung Jüdisches Museum Berlin

Publisher: Stiftung Jüdisches Museum Berlin
Director: Prof. Dr. W. Michael Blumenthal

This book accompanies the Exhibition
of the Jewish Museum Berlin

Project Director Ken Gorbey
Exhibition Design Würth & Winderoll, Seefeld/Munich
Production strand ausstellungsrealisation GmbH

"Stories of an Exhibition"

Text Ingke Brodersen and Rüdiger Dammann, in collaboration
    with the researchers of the Permanent Exhibition

Stories from the Learning Center
Shabbtai Zvi Jan-Christian Schwarz
Rural Jewish Cooking Uri Kaufmann
Tea and Talk—The Berlin Salons Jutta Strauss
Bertha Pappenheim Léontine Meijer and Barbara Rösch
The Judengasse in Frankfurt Jörg H. Fehrs
"Nesthäkchen" and Nationalism Sylvia Rogge-Gau
Eastern Jews in the Ruhr Valley Sibylle Kußmaul
Exile in Shanghai Simone Erpel, Sarah Hiron and Christine Zahn

Tradition and Change Michal Kümper

Architecture Helmuth F. Braun, Head of Temporary Exhibitions
Axes Leonore Maier, Archive Researcher
Gallery of the Missing Ken Gorbey, Project Director
The Collection Inka Bertz, Head of Collections and Research
The Archive of the Leo Baeck Institute Aubrey Pomerance, Head of
    the Archive of the Leo Baeck Institute in the Jewish Museum
    Berlin
Education Cilly Kugelmann, Head of Education
Rafael Roth Learning Center Jutta Strauss, Rafael Roth Learning
    Center Content Leader
Temporary Exhibitions Helmuth F. Braun, Head of Temporary
    Exhibitions
Museum Workshop for the Blind Otto Weidt Kai Gruzdz and
    Ariane Kwasigroch, Researchers Museum Workshop for
    the Blind Otto Weidt

Translation
Text Andrea Scrima
Modernism, Jewish Questions, Present Day Rebecca Morrison
Stories from the Learning Center Ann Robertson
Welcome, The Exhibitions, Gallery of the Missing Miriam Mandelkow
Foreword, Axes, Architecture, Departments of the Museum,
    Quotes and Poems Darrell Wilkins

Editors, Illustrations Signe Rossbach and Kathrin Kollmeier

Cover Hachschara camp Schniebinchen near Sommerfeld
    in the Niederlausitz, ca. 1938, Stiftung Jüdisches Museum
    Berlin, Photograph by Herbert Sonnenfeld

Design, Layout Groothuis, Lohfert, Consorten | glcons.de
Typeset Offizin Götz Gorissen, Berlin
Reproduction EINSATZ Creative Production, Hamburg
Printing Offizin Andersen Nexö Leipzig
Type Legacy (ITC)

We would like to thank the following firms for their financial support
in the production of this book:
EINSATZ Creative Production, Hamburg

Supported by the Federal Government Commissioner of Cultural Affairs
and the Media

ISBN 3-00-008299-9